THE
INFLUENCE
OF THE BIBLE

JOHN MATTHEWS

SOLID GROUND CHRISTIAN BOOKS
BIRMINGHAM, ALABAMA USA

Companion Volume
Published by Solid Ground

THE DIVINE PURPOSE
Displayed in the Works of Providence and Grace

"The chief excellency of these Letters is, that they present the subject of DIVINE DECREES, without the forbidding aspect, which it is apt to assume in the view of many persons. One thing the reader may be assured of, that whether he should coincide in opinion with the author or not, he will find nothing in the volume calculated to wound the most delicate feelings. A spirit of meekness and kindness, eminently characteristic of the writer, pervades the whole." - Archibald Alexander, from the Preface

"John Matthews letters on the Divine Purpose, after being collected into a volume, passed through several editions, and were afterwards issued by the Presbyterian Board of Publication. They have placed their author among the best standard theological writers of the present age." – James Wood, from the Memoir

Retail Price $16.00
ISBN: 978-159925-239-1
205-443-0311
sgcborders@charterinternet.com
www.solid-ground-books.com

THE
INFLUENCE OF THE BIBLE
IN IMPROVING THE
UNDERSTANDING
AND
MORAL CHARACTER

BY
JOHN MATTHEWS, D.D.,
PROFESSOR OF THEOLOGY IN THE THEOLOGICAL SEMINARY
AT HANOVER AND NEW ALBANY, INDIANA
AUTHOR OF
"LETTERS ON THE DIVINE PURPOSE"

WITH A MEMOIR OF THE AUTHOR,
BY JAMES WOOD, D.D.
PRESIDENT OF HANOVER COLLEGE, INDIANA

PHILADELPHIA
PRESBYTERIAN BOARD OF PUBLICATION,
NO. 821 CHESTNUT STREET
1864

Solid Ground Christian Books
PO Box 660132
Vestavia Hills AL 35266
205-443-0311
sgcb@charter.net
solid-ground-books.com

THE INFLUENCE OF THE BIBLE
In Improving the Understanding and Moral Character
by John Matthews (1772-1848)

Taken from the 1864 edition published by
The Presbyterian Board of Publication

First Solid Ground edition February 2010

Cover design by Borgo Design, Tuscaloosa, AL

ISBN: 978-159925-144-8

CONTENTS

MEMOIR OF THE AUTHOR,   5

PART ONE

SECTION I
Self-Examination Improves the Understanding   17

SECTION II
Exhibitions of Wisdom Improve the Understanding   33

SECTION III
Exhibitions of Greatness Improve the Understanding   60

PART TWO

SECTION I
Economy and Industry, Taught in the Bible—
    Promote Human Happiness   79

SECTION II
Intemperance—Importance of Truth, Justice, Honesty—
    Effects of Sinful Passions   102

CONTENTS

SECTION III
Discontentedness, Peevishness; Pious Affections
   Secure Peace of Mind   126

SECTION IV
Meekness, Forbearance, Kindness, &c.,
   Promote Human Happiness   151

SECTION V
The Gospel Furnishes Support in Affliction—
   Influence of Faith, Hope, and Love,   174

SECTION VI
The Religion of the Bible, The True Happiness of Man   195

MEMOIR OF THE AUTHOR.

SOME persons are more influenced by the temporal benefits of the gospel than by those which are spiritual and eternal. To such readers this volume has a special adaptation. It is designed to show that genuine religion, when sincerely embraced and practised, makes men wiser, better, and happier, than others are or can be in similar circumstances, without piety. To this end it maintains that the acquisition and cordial belief of divine knowledge, as revealed in the Bible, improve the understanding, and increase our intellectual strength and vigor; that they refine the heart, control the temper, and regulate the life, and thus form a high moral character; and finally that they produce faith, hope, and love, and by these powerful and appropriate means support and comfort the soul in adversity.

In concluding his discussion on the intellectual benefits of the Bible, our author remarks: "It is readily admitted that among the Greeks and Romans, who were ignorant of divine revelation, there were many whose minds were improved with the knowledge of arts and sciences, in a degree far above thousands of Christians.

This admission, however, does not in the least affect our conclusion. No man will affirm that their minds could not have been improved in a greater degree than they were, by the application of means calculated to produce this effect. We contend that the Bible furnishes these very means, that the knowledge and belief of its truth would have improved their minds in a still greater degree, and have rendered them still more illustrious than they were. If Archimedes had been a sincere and humble and devout Christian, he might have been the Newton of the world. If Socrates, Plato, Aristotle, and Seneca had felt the transforming light and power of the Book of God, they might have filled the place now occupied by Locke, and Reid, and Beattie, and Paley."

No less pertinent and expressive are the author's remarks on the moral effects and tendencies of the Bible, and its power to promote individual and social happiness. "Who," he asks, "can look on the world, agitated and afflicted as it is with these restless and guilty passions," (alluding to avarice, ambition, pride, anger, revenge, intemperance, &c.,) "without breathing to Heaven an ardent desire for some remedy that will restore peace to the mind, and relieve mankind from the evils which they suffer from this source? The Bible is that remedy. No sooner does its divine light shine into the understanding; no sooner does its sacred truth impress the heart, than a change commences, which, in its progress, tends to peace and happiness. The proud man becomes humble; the ambitious man becomes moderate in his expectations and desires; envy and jealousy wither and die with the root which nourishes them; the avaricious man gives up his idol, and raises his affections to God; anger is displaced by meekness; malice, resentment and revenge, by forbearance, the forgiveness of injuries, brotherly-kindness, and charity; the discontented, ill-natured, peevish, murmuring, querulous spirit becomes contented, mild, gentle, good-natured, and benevolent. Destroy these evil passions and tempers, and you prevent all the misery and disquietude which they produce; excite in their stead these friendly and devout affections, and those who cherish them will enjoy peace within, become useful members of society, and contribute, in no small degree, to the happiness of all with whom they are connected." Again, "The most rational consolation and support, the purest joy which man, in this vale of sorrow, can taste; the brightest days which this dark, and miserable, and sinful world will ever witness, will be owing to the influence of the Book of God."

In such terms as these does our author eulogize and recommend the sacred Scriptures. With him his treatise was not a mere theory. We state this from personal acquaintance. It was our privilege to be officially associated with him nine years. Our personal intercourse was also frequent and intimate. We have never known a man, who was a finer specimen of those intellectual, and especially those moral qualities which ennoble and adorn human nature, and show the truth and value of our holy religion.

Dr. Matthews was born in Alamance congregation, not far from Greensboro', Guilford County, N. C., Jan

19, 1772. His ancestors were Irish. His father was not wealthy, and from principle he never owned slaves. His son John's early educational advantages were small, but he manifested a decided taste for intellectual culture ; and while engaged in learning the carpenter's trade, he improved his leisure moments in perusing such books as fell in his way. At the age of nineteen or twenty he sought in good earnest to obtain an education : for which purpose he entered a High School, taught by the Rev. David Caldwell, D. D., and supported himself in part by his trade. During one of his vacations, he aided in finishing a house of public worship, particularly the pulpit, in which, after his licensure, he preached the gospel. His mechanical genius was considerable. He built the carriage in which Dr. Caldwell, Principal of the Academy, was accustomed to ride. He also constructed a planetarium, in which the heavenly bodies were made to revolve. This was done soon after the discovery by Herschel, of the planet Uranus, and before it had been laid down in astronomical charts. But learning from the published accounts of its discovery, the plane of its orbit, he, by the aid of his mathematical knowledge, gave it its true position in his miniature firmament.

Dr. Matthews obtained his entire education, literary and theological, in Dr. Caldwell's school. "His school," says Dr. Foote, in his Sketches of North Carolina, " was the means, during the long period of its continuance, of bringing more men into the learned professions than any others taught by a single individual, or by a succession of teachers during the same period of time. Five

MEMOIR OF THE AUTHOR.

of his scholars became governors of States; a number were promoted to the bench," .... " a larger number, it is supposed about fifty, became ministers of the gospel, of whom were" .... " Dr. John Matthews, of New Albany, Ind., Dr. Brown, of Tennessee, and many others who were shining lights." ....
" Most, if not all of those whose names have been mentioned as eminent, received their entire classical education from him, and the ministers of the gospel, in addition to that, their theological education; so that for a time his school was Academy, College, and Theological Seminary. The number of students attending was generally from fifty to sixty."

Dr. Matthews was "licensed to preach by the Presbytery of Orange, in March, 1801, being in his thirtieth year." See Dr. Sprague's Annals of the American Pulpit, from which this and some other facts are taken, although most of our statements are derived from original sources. In the autumn after his licensure, he went on a missionary tour to the State of Mississippi, which was then new and uncultivated. We have heard him speak modestly of his severe exposures, privations, and perils, during that tour. He said that " he accomplished, as he hoped, some good, and derived personal benefit, by his salutary discipline, preparatory to the duties and trials which God designed for him in after life."

In 1803 he became pastor of the Nutbush and Grassy Creek churches, in Granville county, N. C., where he remained till 1806. In 1805 and 1806, two successive years, he was sent by his Presbytery as a commissioner to the General Assembly, which circumstance, it is probable, led to his forming an acquaintance with the church in Martinsburg, Va., from which he received a call in 1806. Having accepted their call, he removed from North Carolina to that place; but in less than two years he removed again, and became the stated supply of the churches of Shepherdstown and Charlestown, Va., to which he ministered with fidelity, acceptableness, and success, for seventeen or eighteen years; after which he gave up his charge at Shepherdstown, and divided his time between Charlestown and Martinsburg, till his removal to the West in 1830. How highly he was esteemed as a pastor, may be inferred from the fact that about ten years prior to his decease, he being then sixty-seven years of age, a period when ministers were not often as popular as in early life, the church at Charlestown invited him to resume his pastoral labours among them.

In 1823 he received the honorary degree of D. D., from Washington College, Pa.

His removal to the West in 1830, was occasioned by a call to the professorship of Theology in a Theological Seminary about to be commenced at Hanover, Indiana, by the name of the Indiana Theological Seminary, and under the supervision of the Synod of Indiana. He was inaugurated in June, 1831. There was established by that Synod, at the same time and place, a Literary Institution, which, in 1832, was chartered as Hanover College; an institution which has educated wholly or in part about three thousand students, some eight hundred of whom have become ministers of the gospel.

Hanover was then new; most of the western country was new, and the pecuniary resources of the College and Theological Seminary were inadequate to sustain the professors, except by the most rigid and self-denying economy. For several years the two institutions were closely connected together, and Dr. Matthews gave instruction in both; acting also, from 1836 to 1838, as president *pro tem.* of the college. He resided at Hanover till 1840, when, on the removal of the Theological Seminary to New Albany, he changed his residence to that place, and continued there until his decease. This change in the location of the seminary resulted from a desire of the Synod of Indiana to secure the co-operation of the other western Synods, for which purpose a convention was called, composed of delegates from several Synods, to deliberate on the subject, and to decide by a majority of votes at what point the seminary should be established. New Albany was fixed upon as the location, at which place it assumed the name of the New Albany Theological Seminary, and was carried on under the control of from four to seven Synods, until 1857, when it was removed again to Chicago, Ill., with another change of name to the Theological Seminary of the Northwest. In 1859, it was placed under the care of the General Assembly, and it is now conducted under the supervision of that body. In anticipation of the removal of the seminary from Hanover, the Library, which belonged jointly to the College and Theological Seminary, was divided, and twenty-six hundred volumes, a portion of which had been collected by Dr. Matthews, were conveyed to

New Albany. Many of these volumes were large and valuable standard works, some of them old and rare ; to which additions were subsequently made of about one thousand volumes more, and the whole now compose a part of the library of the Theological Seminary of the Northwest, at Chicago.

Dr. Matthews resided at Hanover nine years, and at New Albany eight. He departed this life at the latter place, May 19, 1848, in the 77th year of his age. His end was peace. We conversed with him several times on the subject of personal religion, during the last few days of his life; the last time about an hour before his decease. In one of these conversations allusion was made to Solomon's description of old age, in the 12th chapter of Ecclesiastes. He remarked, "That description suits my case; the machine is nearly run down; worn out;" and added, to the effect, that in the heavenly state, our resurrection bodies will be restored to perfect health and vigour, never again to suffer decay.

As a man, Dr. Matthews possessed talents of a high order. His reasoning powers were acute, his judgment sound, and his mind well balanced and well cultivated. His knowledge was extensive, and in some departments he was a profound scholar. Few excelled him in clearness of metaphysical discussion, and his familiarity with the original language of the New Testament was remarkable. To the very close of his life he could quote with ease many of the most important words, and give a critical exposition of their import.

But his moral and religious character exceeded his intellectual. Ordinarily he was rather taciturn, but when called out, his conversational powers were good, and his words were uniformly seasoned with salt. He was pleasant, but never light and trifling. He did not speak or act precipitately or rashly, but with suitable deliberation and caution, and a due regard to the proprieties of the case. He never spoke evil concerning his neighbours. He therefore neither kindled the flame of discord, nor fanned and kept it alive after it had been kindled by others. On the contrary, he "followed peace with all men," and seldom, if ever, failed to "live peaceably with all." His language and conduct were invariably so kind and sincere, as to produce the general impression that he was "an Israelite indeed, in whom there was no guile." He was also so meek as to disarm those who might otherwise have been disposed to be disrespectful or insulting. He never rendered evil for evil, and if he ever felt anger rising in his heart, he always suppressed it before it became visible in his countenance. We learned from one who knew him in early life, that these qualities were not natural, but acquired; partly by much self-discipline, and still more by divine grace. His piety was not impulsive, but practical; not fluctuating, now joyful, and then melancholy; but constant and regular in its manifestation as the return of day.

Some traits in his character may be seen more clearly by a few incidents. He was remarkable for punctuality in meeting his appointments; but his watch occasionally failed to keep good time. When, as a consequence of this failure, he was sometimes too late, he would remark,

"My watch is not a moral agent." His manner of reproving sin, though effective, seldom gave offence. When officiating as President *pro tempore* of Hanover College, he heard a student use profane language, while engaged in chopping a stick of wood. Dr. Matthews took the axe from his hands, cut the wood in two pieces, and then remarked to the young man, " You perceive that a stick of wood can be cut in two without swearing." He had a strong aversion to any appendage which was worn for show, and not from necessity or utility. When he was about seventy years old, a friend presented him with a cane. He thanked him for the offer, but declined its acceptance, saying, " When I am old enough, sir, to need a cane, I will gladly accept your gift."

As a preacher, Dr. Matthews was always listened to with attention and interest, though he would not be called a pulpit orator. Owing to a trembling in his hands, he employed his pen but little during the last eighteen or twenty years of his life. Hence we never heard him preach a written discourse. But he spoke with fluency, though not rapidly; and he was so accurate in the use of terms, that he seldom recalled a word after it was uttered, or had any occasion to change it for another, better adapted to express his meaning. He addressed the understanding rather than the imagination. Hence he did not abound in rhetorical figures. He used to counsel his students not to go out of their way to gather flowers; but to use them moderately, if they found them in their path, and when their use would elucidate the sense or increase the power of their sermons. He was an earnest preacher, but not impassioned; edifying and impressive, but not often, though occasionally, pathetic. His pathos, when it occurred, was no studied effort to touch the sensibilities of his audience, but the spontaneous effusion of his own heart, moved by the tenderness of his subject, and in these cases his hearers were often melted to tears. When he attended ecclesiastical bodies, it was always expected that he would preach once at least during the meeting; and though he did not put himself forward, he never declined performing the service, when, by the appointment of the Presbytery or Synod, it became, as he thought, his duty. In the discussions which arose in the body, during the progress of business, he often remained silent, while his juniors in age and experience were permitted to take a leading part; but when his voice was heard, his manner was characterized by simplicity and sincerity, and his matter by good sense and sound wisdom.

As a professor of theology, Dr. Matthews was able and diligent. For the reason already mentioned, he did not write his lectures in full; but they were thoroughly digested, and highly satisfactory to the students. He commenced the year with a brief course on Mental Philosophy; and this was succeeded by didactic, polemic, and pastoral theology, together with the composition and delivery of sermons; in all of which his instructions would compare favourably with those given on the same subjects at any other theological seminary in our country.

As an author, Dr. Matthews published far less than he would have done under other circumstances. He once remarked pleasantly, in our hearing, that, "if it had not been for this trembling hand, which unfitted him for holding a pen, the world would probably have been afflicted with more of his writings than was now the case." Except his Inaugural Address, at Hanover, in 1831, and a sermon contributed to a " Volume of Sermons by Presbyterian Ministers in the Mississippi Valley," in 1833, with a few short articles for religious periodicals, he published nothing, we believe, after his removal to the West. From 1812 to 1826, his publications consisted of seven occasional sermons, and two series of articles in the " Literary and Theological Magazine," edited by Dr. John H. Rice, of Richmond, Va., entitled " Letters on the Divine Purpose," and " The Influence of the Bible, in improving the Understanding and Moral Character." His letters on the Divine Purpose, after being collected into a volume, passed through several editions, and were afterwards issued by the Presbyterian Board of Publication. They have placed their author among the best standard theological writers of the present age. His articles on the Influence of the Bible, now issued by the same Board, were first republished in a volume in 1833. Its circulation has been limited, but it only requires to become as well known as the other volume just mentioned, in order to make it as highly appreciated. The two together, like the two pillars, Jachin and Boaz, in Solomon's temple, are strong and valuable supports in the temple of truth, and a fitting memorial of a man whose talents, learning, piety, and usefulness entitle him to be held in lasting remembrance.

JAMES WOOD.

HANOVER, Ind., October 5, 1863.

THE INFLUENCE OF THE BIBLE.

PART I.

SECTION I.

Self-examination improves the understanding.

THE great design of the Bible is to qualify men for the life to come; yet in producing this effect, it is pleasing to know and observe the direct and powerful tendency which it possesses and exerts in qualifying them for respectability and usefulness in this life. When it is understood and received in the love of it, the character, both intellectual and moral, will be improved; and under its influence and its guidance, those habits will be formed on which the happiness and prosperity of civil society very much depend. If it could be divested of its spiritual tendencies, of its influence in producing that *holiness, without which no man shall see the Lord*, it is still worthy of our grateful acknowledgment on account of its numerous and benign effects on human life.

It will contribute very much to the improvement of the understanding. The mind, as well as the body, will acquire habits from the frequent repetition of the same exercises. Those parts of the body which are employed in the performance of work, requiring strength, will acquire an enlargement and firmness of muscle, fitting them for the task, which, without this exercise they would not possess, and which will render them rather disproportionate to the other parts of the same body. Instances of this kind come under the observation of every person. Such is also the case with the mind; its vigour and enlargement depend very much on its habitual exercise. If circumstances confine its operations to but few objects, and these requiring but little intellectual effort to understand them, the mind will be contracted in its capacity, and feeble in its powers. But if the objects about which it is employed are diversified and difficult of comprehension, the mind will become enlarged, and its faculties will be strengthened. Some minds, indeed, possess a native, restless, irrepressible vigour which will burst through the restraints thrown around it by the most unfavourable circumstances. You might as well expect to suppress the subterranean fountains from bursting forth, and urging their way to the wide ocean, or to quiet that ocean with a word, as to expect that such a mind will rest till it finds its own element: it will struggle, it will rise until it reaches a theatre presenting it with objects which will give it, at once, employment, delight, and improvement. In general, however, the intellectual character of man depends on the circumstances with which he is surrounded. The objects to which the mind is habitually applied impart to it something of their own character. If they are few and simple, they will contract and enfeeble the mind; if numerous and complicated, they will enlarge and strengthen it; if grand and sublime, they will give it a pleasing elevation and expansion.

For this reason classical studies should hold their place in literary institutions. They are valuable, not on account of the useful and practical information which they furnish, but for the mental discipline which they give; for the habits of discrimination and logical reasoning which the student acquires; habits which cannot fail to be highly useful in every department of life, in every exercise of the understanding. For this reason the science of astronomy is always delightful and improving; the order, the connection, the grandeur of the objects embraced in this study cannot fail to elevate and expand the mind.

On this principle it is, we affirm that the Bible will improve the intellectual character of the Christian. The objects which it presents to his consideration, and about which his thoughts must be, with more or less interest, employed, are numerous, complicated, and beyond conception grand and sublime. Their number will give variety to the exercise of his mind; their complex nature will increase the power of discrimination, and strengthen the reasoning faculty; their infinite magnitude and importance, their attractive majesty and glory will give a conscious and pleasing elevation and enlargement to the whole soul.

The Christian is required to be *ready always to give an answer to every man that asketh him, a reason of the hope that is in him, with meekness and fear.* This implies that all genuine religious hope is supported by certain reasons, or evidence, with which he is to become acquainted, and which he is to ascertain, not by intuition, nor by miracle, nor by any immediate revelation from God, but by frequently and closely investigating his own heart, with all its varied and complicated exercises and emotions. He is also required to examine himself whether he be in the faith, to know and to prove himself. Examination, with a view to a correct decision, implies the comparison of various things with each other, and with some acknowledged standard. Were there no spurious exercises of a religious nature, none which so nearly resemble the true, as, without the strictest investigation, to endanger the great interests of the soul, this examination would be unnecessary. But this is not the case; there are such spurious exercises of the heart: every feature of the Christian character has its counterfeit. The object of examination is to discriminate between the spurious and the genuine exercise, between the true feature and its mere resemblance. He is to examine whether his faith be the living word of God, with all its energies, transferred and rooted in the soul, working by love, purifying the heart, overcoming the world; or a mere painting of fancy, nothing but the images and workings of the imagination, or nothing but a collection of ideas, without any transforming effect on the heart and on the life. The true Christian loves God. But he is not to admit, without impartial inquiry, that every motion which he feels, that every joyous glow which warms his heart, is that love. He must ascertain whether its principle is selfish, or spiritual and generous; whether it regards the whole character of God, displayed through the cross of Christ in the salvation of sinners, or merely what is supposed to be the mercy of God, but which in truth is little more than a human weakness, and especially whether it leaves him satisfied with a partial observance of only some few precepts of the gospel, or by its holy and ceaseless workings, prompts him to sincere and uniform obedience to all the will of God, to the whole system of Christian duty. He is to love his fellow-christians, not because they hold the same creed, and belong to the same denomination with himself, but because they bear the image of their common Saviour. In like manner, every other affection of his heart is to be submitted to the same scrutiny; his repentance, gratitude, meekness, &c.

In this investigation he not only compares these feelings with each other, but he compares them with the word of God, which he adopts as the standard, the only infallible Judge in such cases. There he learns the nature of all affections truly devout; there he learns the effect they will have on the temper of his mind, and on his life; he there hears the voice of the Spirit, testifying what are the characteristic features of a child of God. With this he compares the witness of his own spirit, obtained by this careful investigation; if they agree together, he concludes that he is a child of God. On this concurrent testimony of his own spirit and the spirit of God his hope rests as its foundation; this is the reason which he is ready to give for the hope which he entertains of acceptance with God, and of final salvation.

Again; although the precepts of the Bible are remarkable for their plainness and extent, yet a thousand cases will occur for which there is no explicit direction. To expect this in the Bible would be most unreasonable; such instructions would swell the volume to a useless size. Circumstances may often surround the Christian, in which he is compelled to act, which require much deliberation to discover what course he ought to pursue. In this state he is often conscious of painful suspense; and, if permitted, would offer up the prayer that a voice from heaven would decide the doubtful case, or that a pillar of cloud would move in the direction he ought to take. Neither voice nor cloud, however, decides the case. Inclination may prove an unsafe guide, and lead him widely astray. He must consider, he must compare, he must reason, he must judge for himself where the path of duty lies. He will keep in view the great principles of Christian morals laid down in the gospel; he will consider what aid can be derived from the example of the Saviour; he will reflect on the tendency of the proposed course, the effect it will probably have on others, and on the interests of the church; he will especially anticipate, as near as possible, the decision of his omniscient Judge. Thus he will deliberate; and finally take that course for which there is the greatest weight of reason, which he judges to be upon the whole, best. Sometimes as he advances, he is more and more cheered with the conviction that his decision was correct, that he escaped from his difficulties by the right direction; sometimes he advances with painful hesitancy; and sometimes he is convinced that, though honest in his inquiries, yet he was mistaken in his conclusion.

Now we maintain that this is as real a process of reasoning as the acquisition of language, or the study of science; and that it is as well calculated to improve the intellectual faculties as either of these are. The method of reasoning, and of reaching the conclusion, as far as the nature of the case will admit, is the method of Newton. That great philosopher took nothing for granted which could be tested by experiment; he built no theories on mere conjecture, drew no important conclusions from mere assumption. His conclusions were derived from principles well established; while evidence derived from experiments, from analogy, and from induction, supported his principles. This is the method of the Christian; he takes nothing for granted; his conclusions do not rest on mere assumption or conjecture. He has the advantage of an experience both extensive and diversified. His whole life is a scene of trials; and every trial brings his principles to the test of experience. By this experience he obtains much valuable knowledge, becomes wiser, and better qualified for future usefulness. The conclusion that he is a child of God, and his hope of acceptance, rest on the evidence of induction from a number of particulars. Indeed this is as complete an exemplification of this method as can be found in the whole range of philosophy. His faith, his love, his repentance, his gratitude, &c., are all examined separately; but his conclusion and his hope do not rest on the evidence furnished by either of these alone; but on that furnished by all of them combined. Newton, convinced that every effect must have an adequate cause, often discovered the cause by considering the effect: and having ascertained the nature and properties of the cause, with safety, inferred the effect which would result from its operation. This is pre-eminently the method of the Christian. He who believes that the grass and the flowers of the field receive their nicest tints and diversified hues of colouring from the pencil of divine skill, that a sparrow cannot fall to the ground without the special design of Heaven, cannot, and does not believe that the devout affections and pious dispositions of his heart are the result of chance or of accident. All these affections are distinctly traced to the word of God, as their instrumental cause. The rejoicing of his hope is produced by the doctrine of the atonement; the love which warms his heart and cheers his journey through life is kindled by the truth, that *God is love;* that reverence which bows his soul within him is the effect of beholding the majesty and holiness of the Great Jehovah.

Having learned the nature and tendency of this truth, he calculates with certainty on all the various and happy effects it will produce on the minds of others. This conclusion inspires him with zeal to diffuse the knowledge of this truth through the earth, and to bring all men to feel its power in reforming the heart and the life. When he hears of the repentance of a sinner, even in the remotest corner of the earth, on the principles of analogy, he knows what those feelings are, and by what means they are excited. Newton sometimes generalized; that is, ascribed various effects to the same cause. The planets, so various in magnitude and the velocity with which they move, at such immense distances from each other and from their common centre, are bound together in one complete and harmonious system by the principle of attraction. This same principle holds together the particles of this earth, gives to it its solidity and figure, and causes all the detached bodies with which it is surrounded to adhere to its surface. This same principle of attraction unites together, with more or less firmness of cohesion, the particles of every species, and every separate piece of matter. This great principle pervades, unites, and governs, subordinate to the design of the Supreme Ruler, the whole material universe, from the sun in the centre, to the remotest planet which revolves around him, even to the wandering comet which flies off into distant regions, where human observation cannot reach. Every species and shape which matter assumes, from the mightiest globe to the smallest atom, feel and obey its power. How striking is the analogy between this attraction and the Christian's faith! Jesus Christ is the sun and centre of the Christian system, of the moral universe. All Christians are united to him by faith; by the same faith they are united to each other. They may live in ages and in regions of this world widely remote from each other; but united by this principle, they are members of one body, are formed into one system, compose one family. By the same faith, through the atoning blood of a Divine Saviour, they obtain the pardon of sin, acceptance and reconciliation with God. While this faith pervades and unites the whole system, it operates, in the hands of God the Spirit, with vital and transforming energy in the heart of each individual. By the word of God, the knowledge and belief of which is faith, the soul is begotten, or quickened, when dead in trespasses and in sins, is roused from a state of insensibility, the first impression of spiritual things is made, a new direction is given to the thoughts, and a new impulse to the feelings. By the word of God the Christian is born again; by faith his heart is purified; by faith he walks, or regulates his life; by faith he sees and feels the importance of spiritual realities; by faith he overcomes the world; by the power of God through faith he is kept unto salvation. The effects of attraction in the material system are not more numerous, important, and diversified, than are those of faith in the Christian system. In perfect accordance with the design of Him *who worketh all things after the counsel of his own will,* this principle unites all the countless millions of the redeemed to each other and to Christ, through whom it obtains their pardon and acceptance with God; in each individual, separately, its reforming energy is felt; all the faculties of his soul, all the affections of his heart, all the ceaseless workings and movements of his thoughts, feel its purifying and decisive control. Newton, on every side, and at no great distance, met with barriers over which he could not pass, beyond which his investigations could not with success be carried. He assured his disciples that there existed, in the material universe, a principle which he called *attraction;* but that he could not define to them the abstract principle, otherwise than by its effects. He told them that there were properties of matter so recondite as to baffle all his efforts to detect and describe them. When he came to these barriers, with a noble modesty, he acknowledged his inability to proceed further: he would not amuse their credulity with mere conjectures respecting the dark regions, forbidden to human inquiry. This acknowledgment evinces the greatness of his mind as clearly as do the numerous and important discoveries which he made. Yet on this account his system is not rejected. The facts which he ascertained by experiment, the principles which he illustrated and proved from their effects, are all admitted and received. The Christian also states his facts, ascertained from numerous and various experiments; he offers, in support of his principles, illustrations and proofs, as satisfactory to the candid mind as those of mathematics. Within certain limits his vision and his comprehension are clear; beyond those limits, he acknowledges there are some things incomprehensible. He believes in the existence and operations of the Holy Spirit, though he can comprehend neither his existence nor the manner of his operations. He feels and he witnesses important and numerous effects which he ascribes to this agency, and for which this belief furnishes a satisfactory account. Why should the *wisdom of this world* show itself by rejecting this system or any part of it, for reasons which bear with equal, if not greater force against the Newtonian system? Why should more be expected from the advocate of Christianity than is expected from Newton? In both systems there is a series of well authenticated facts; in both there are many things perceived and comprehended with sufficient clearness to answer all useful purposes; in both are some things incomprehensible, which can be known only by their effects. Let both systems be viewed with the same unjaundiced eye, and modesty will induce these *wise men* to admit and receive both. Finally; Newton laid down *first principles* from which he never departed; and which aided and guided him in all his investigations. By these he catechized every new phenomenon which met his observation, until he ascertained its origin, the cause by which it was produced, and the class to which it belonged. If once satisfied on these particulars, the fact or the discovery was laid up for usefulness in future, as occasion might require. But if no satisfactory account could be obtained, the matter is left for the present, and no use is made of it. Thus he proceeded with safety, and made those large additions to the stock of useful knowledge which have crowned his name with deserved and lasting renown. The Bible contains the *first principles* of the Christian. By these he is directed and aided in all his inquiries; examines all the aspects which religion assumes; all the various and conflicting opinions and customs which prevail in this mutable world; tries the exercises of his own heart, and the actions of his own life; judges the profession and the life of others. In this balance he weighs the world that now is, and that which is to come. All that meets the approbation of this judge, he receives and treasures up for usefulness in future; that which appears doubtful, he lets remain for farther consideration; that which is condemned, he utterly rejects and avoids. Hence he loves this book, and esteems it more precious than treasures of gold. Thus he advances along the journey of life, passes through its temptations and its snares; bears its afflictions and trials with safety; and thus he will receive, if not the admiration and applause of this world, what is infinitely more important, the blessing and approbation of God, his Judge.

Such is the field of investigation presented to the Christian, and such the exercise furnished to his understanding in proving himself, in keeping his heart, in guarding against deception, in building himself up in the comfort of hope, in ascertaining the path of his duty. Nor is this exercise of the intellect, this process of reasoning, to be carried on merely for a day or a year; but for every day and every year of his life. Every day the movements of his heart are to be watched and examined; every day the path of duty is to be sought and pursued through all the perplexing and changing circumstances which may diversify his life. Without this he cannot feel that joy and peace which cheer and encourage him to persevere; he cannot be useful to the church; he deserves not the name of Christian.

Now we think it evidently appears, that if the study of philosophy, according to the principles of Newton, is calculated to improve the understanding, so is the study of the Bible, more especially when it thoroughly penetrates the soul with its living power. The Christian may know nothing of philosophy, or of its principles; yet in working out his own salvation, his inquiries and his conclusions are according to these principles. He does not make these inquiries and pursue this course with the design of improving his intellectual faculties; the improvement of his heart is the great object; yet in pursuing this purpose, his understanding is necessarily exercised in such a manner, as cannot fail to improve it. Thousands may be engaged in the study of philosophy, whose object is not the improvement of the mind, but to qualify themselves for usefulness, to gain a subsistence, or to gratify their own taste or inclination; yet from such study, the mind will necessarily derive improvement. It is not the design of the industrious mechanic to enlarge and strengthen those parts of the body which are habitually employed; yet this will be the result of such employment. By this discipline the faculty of perception will be quickened, the power of discrimination and correct decision will be strengthened. The Christian may know nothing of the name or the meaning of metaphysics; but he is in reality a metaphysician. He is habitually employed about abstract ideas, addressed, not to his senses, but to his understanding. Mind, and its operations, engage his close and constant attention. Thus while his object is to prepare himself for heaven, to secure for himself a crown of life, his understanding brightens and improves by the means which he uses to gain that high and holy purpose.

SECTION II.

Exhibitions of Wisdom improve the understanding.

Exhibitions of wisdom, in harmonizing real and apparent discordancies, and arranging and bringing into operation a series of means for the accomplishment of some great and good purpose, always furnish a pleasing and improving exercise to the understanding. In considering such displays, we make more or less effort to follow the operations of that mind whose wisdom we behold, in its deliberations, its arrangements, and designs. If there is hope of success in the attempt, we exert our understanding to comprehend these operations, and thus to equal the wisdom which we contemplate; or if this appears impracticable, we admire that greatness which we can neither equal nor comprehend. Such efforts will never fail to improve the mind which makes them.

That the material creation displays, in a high degree, the wisdom of God, is universally admitted. Every part of matter, animate and inanimate, from the insect of an hour, to the mightiest orb that pursues its majestic round in the heavens, manifests a wisdom worthy of the great Creator. But while this is readily admitted, we affirm, without hesitation, because we solemnly believe it, that the cross of Christ furnishes a display of wisdom as much greater than this, as the heavens are higher than the earth, as mind is superior to matter. In its finest and purest state, matter is too gross to receive and display the greatest exhibitions of wisdom: an intelligent being, a moral agent, alone can answer this purpose. From the hands of an artist, a block of wood may receive the shape, but never can receive the polish of the finest marble, or the purest metal. In the material creation, there is nothing but mere inert, unresisting matter to arrange and to govern: but in the moral world, there is intellect, with its own designs and decisions to manage; there is thought to guide; there is passion, affection, and disposition to control. An artist can give form and proportion, and almost breath and animation, to the marble and to the canvass. But the marble has no design of its own to change and to govern, makes no objection, offers no opposition to his will; the colours form no scheme to thwart and disappoint his design, but dwell on the canvass in that proportion of light and shade, which he is pleased to give them. But how widely different, and how much more difficult is the task, to form a moral character after a given pattern! Let the experiment be made on a child, and let it commence from the very cradle. Let the pattern after which it is to be formed be taken from the world; one whose heart is untouched and unreformed by the gospel: one of the best specimens of morality without vital piety. In accomplishing this task, it is not unintelligent, unresisting matter that is to be formed and proportioned; but there is an intelligent being, an unfolding mind, with all its own views, conclusions, and designs to manage: here is a ceaseless flow of thought to direct, and direct too at every hour; here springing up from within, are passions, desires, hopes, and fears, combined in a thousand diversified forms and degrees, to control. All parents who have been faithful to their children; all instructors of youth, who are worthy the useful and honourable station which they fill, will anticipate much that might be said on this subject; and will unite in declaring, as the result of their experience, that the task is extremely difficult, and, in most cases, surpassed their utmost skill and perseverance. Still more difficult would it be to change a character already formed after a model, the reverse of that which you would wish it to be. Seldom, indeed, does the wisdom and benevolence of man succeed in this attempt. The hard lessons of adversity, the recoil of past folly and imprudence, sometimes effect considerable changes for the better. But, in general, the character thus formed remains and is confirmed to the last. The thoughts and passions, the most essential features of moral character, with extreme reluctance forsake their accustomed channel, to flow in one entirely new. To form the character of a child after the model of the gospel, is as much more difficult than the former case, as the morality of the gospel is more pure and more perfect than that of the world. In this attempt, insurmountable obstacles meet and frustrate the best directed efforts of human agency. Most of all is it difficult to change a character, formed and confirmed by the practice and indulgence of many years in vice and sin, and bring it to bear the image of Jesus Christ. Among the best efforts which man can make with this view, are his humble confessions of utter inability, and his earnest prayers for that divine power which alone can answer this purpose. Now, this is the very change which the gospel proposes, and which the gospel accomplishes, in every case where it is cordially received.

While, therefore, the world of matter gives bright and striking displays of the divine wisdom, far brighter and more striking are the displays of that wisdom, furnished in the cross of Christ. The gospel is truly and emphatically the *wisdom of God*. We admire the wisdom of creation; we more than admire, we adore, the wisdom of redemption.

Every department of nature will amply repay the diligent student of her mysteries with the improvement of his understanding, and with the benefits to mankind which often result from his investigations. The physician has a field of inquiry more than sufficient to engage his attention through life, in the anatomy and diseases of the human body, and in the nature and properties of those remedies which he provides for these diseases. The metaphysician and the moralist are the physicians of the mind; they dissect its parts, arrange its faculties and its powers, point out its diseases, and prescribe the remedies for these diseases. The astronomer bounds from the surface of this little earth to the remotest planet, measures its distance and its magnitude, calculates its orbit and its velocity. He chases the comet in its retrograde flight, till it disappears and leaves him gazing on empty space. He turns his view to the faintest star which can be made to twinkle on his eye through the best optical instrument. Aided by analogy, he surrounds each of these luminous points with a system of revolving planets, like that to which he belongs. Each of these behold, with admiration and delight, the wisdom of God—the astronomer, on a grander scale, but not in more diversified forms, nor in clearer displays, than the anatomist. The Christian, without neglecting these studies, takes his stand at the cross of a Divine Saviour; there, with devout adoration and the purest delight, he beholds the brightest displays of divine wisdom that ever were made to intelligent beings.

The object proposed is not only great and good, but the greatest and the best—the glory of God, the manifestation of his own infinite excellence. This purpose is answered, in part, by the work of creation; but in a much higher degree, by the work of redemption. The power, wisdom, and goodness of God, are exhibited in creation; in addition to these, the mercy, compassion, and forbearance of God, are displayed in the salvation of sinners. None but intelligent creatures, or moral agents, can be guilty, for they alone can transgress a moral law; and none but the guilty can be objects of mercy, compassion, and forbearance. Matter, therefore, in its sublimest order and arrangement, in its most complex organization, never could be the channel of communication for these divine perfections. In the cross of Christ alone they are displayed, and surround the character of Deity with its mildest majesty and most attractive glory. What will be the character of the new heavens and the new earth, mentioned in Scripture, we cannot tell; but the heavens and the earth which we now behold are doomed to change, and to pass away. But every sinner, redeemed by the blood of Christ, shall remain an everlasting monument of the wisdom as well as the mercy of God.

Wisdom is perceived not only in the object which it proposes, but also in the appointment and arrangement of means adapted to the accomplishment of this object. Here we are lost in pious astonishment at the displays of infinite wisdom in these arrangements. There are numerous and diversified series of means, involving each other, connected with each other, and subordinate to each other.

The first series is in subordination to the great and ultimate object. With regard to the second series, the first is a primary object, for the accomplishment of which the second is wisely adapted. The second, while it operates in subordination to the first, is, with regard to the third, a primary object, for the promotion of which the arrangements of the third are made. The third series again is a primary object with regard to the fourth, and the fourth to the fifth, and so on through the whole gradation. The fifth, by promoting the fourth, promotes the third, and thus also the second, and the first, and ultimately the great pre-eminent purpose. Take away the fifth, and the fourth will not answer the intended purpose; for want of the fourth, the third will be deprived of its energy; the second, of course, will be affected for want of the third; and the first again for want of the second; and thus the great object will be prevented by the failure of any part of those means on the operation of which it depends for its accomplishment. The wisdom of God, however, has effectually guarded against the possibility of any such failure. Every series, and every part of that series, operates in perfect order and at the proper time. Nothing is premature; nothing is tardy; nothing is excessive; nothing is deficient. Thus a great system is formed embracing a vast concatenation of causes and effects, all converging to one point, all promoting one grand object.

The death of Jesus Christ was necessary, as far as we can judge, as the means of displaying the divine glory in the salvation of sinners. This harmonized the justice and mercy of God, and thus furnishes a very striking exhibition of the wisdom of Deity. Before their union was demonstrated by this event, they might have been supposed irreconcilable. Mercy can only be exercised in the pardon of sin; but sin deserves punishment; and justice requires the infliction of deserved punishment. The sinner cannot be pardoned, if he suffers the demerit of his crimes; for pardon is deliverance from such punishment. In the cross these apparently discordant attributes unite in perfect harmony; and by their union increase the glory of each other: God is just as well as merciful, in the pardon of sin.

While the death of Christ is the means of manifesting the divine glory, it is itself a great object, to which a vast variety of arrangements are subordinate. Had man, by his wisdom, been required to fix on the proper time for this event, he would probably have erected the cross immediately after the fall. Let the remedy, he would probably have said, be provided and be known, as soon as the disease is felt. Let the knowledge of the atonement descend and spread with the descending and spreading contagion of sin. The wisdom of God, however, determined otherwise. For many ages, but few and faint intimations of his merciful designs were given; and the world was left to make a grand experi ent on its own principles—an experiment which we need not wish to see repeated. The wickedness of men became so great, that even the patience of God could tolerate them no longer on the earth: they were swept off by the deluge. That period at which the crucifixion of the Saviour was to take place, is called, in Scripture, *the fulness of time;* that is, when the world was prepared for it. Either sooner or later, there is reason to believe, would not so well have answered the purpose in view. Expectation was to be excited. With this view, Abraham was called; the Jews were separated; the ceremonial law was given, every rite and offering of which had a reference, more or less direct, to Christ: these were the shadows, he was the substance. Thus expectation of his advent was excited and confirmed. Holy prophets were to predict the manner of his birth, his life, and his death, and the glorious consequences which should follow. This expectation is not only confirmed, but kindles into desire and hope. The nations are to be overturned, to prepare the way of the Lord. Then, and not till then, the wisdom of God determined that the Saviour should die; when it would make the best impression on the world, produce the most glorious effects through time and through eternity.

Christ having died, this fact is to be made known to the world—another grand object for the accomplishment of which a variety of circumstances offer their concurrent operation. The fulness of time, no doubt, had a reference to this event, which was to commence immediately after the death of the Saviour. During many preceding ages, a succession of events had been taking place, to bring the world into that state most favourable to the promulgation of the gospel. Kingdoms had risen and fallen in succession, like waves of the ocean, till at this time the Roman empire embraced in its limits what was then called the whole world. The Old Testament had long been translated into the Greek language; the polite and learned language of that day. The Jews, carrying the Scripture with them, were dispersed in every province, and in almost every city and village of the whole empire. They built their synagogues, or had their appointed places where prayer was wont to be made. Every one must see what facilities this state of things furnished to the first heralds of the cross. Everywhere they found a synagogue, or a place of prayer to which they resorted; they found Jews, their own countrymen, to whom they made their first proclamations of mercy; they found the oracles of God which they read and expounded, and out of which they reasoned, proving that Jesus was the Messiah, foretold and expected by the old prophets. This opened their way to the Gentiles, to whom they offered salvation. If any of these circumstances had been wanting, great, if not insuperable difficulties would have been met in preaching the gospel. The wisdom, then, of this whole arrangement is obvious and striking, and cannot fail to impress all attentive observers.

The first preachers of the gospel were to be selected and prepared for the duties of their office. Much more depends on the wisdom of this choice, than will meet the view of superficial observers. The office is the most important that can be filled by man. If ever the gospel required faithful men, who were able to teach others, it required them now. For several years after the death of Christ, during which the gospel was extensively made known, there was no written account of the life and doctrines of the Saviour; no record of undoubted authority, to which, as to an infallible judge, doubtful cases in doctrine and practice could be referred for decision. No part of the New Testament was then written. The want of such a record would make a very great difference. If an error in doctrine is now advanced, we have our Bible at hand; we can turn to the passage which refutes that error. If any thing criminal in practice appears, we can point out the precept which condemns that practice. How different would be the case, if all such decisions depended on the mere opinion and authority of men! And when the first narrative was written, for want of the art of printing, its circulation must have been very limited, compared with what it might have been by the aid of this art. The truth and genuineness of the gospel depended on the knowledge and fidelity of its first preachers. During these years the apostles and first preachers were to the churches and to all men, what the New Testament is to us—the supreme authority in doctrine and practice. The gospel was to make its first impression on the world; and it was highly important that this should be a just impression. This work required men of sound minds, of accurate and extensive knowledge in all things relating to their office, and especially of deep and ardent piety. Such were the men selected by the wisdom of God for this important purpose. Of this fact, their preaching and their writings, which have come to our knowledge, furnish the most ample testimony. True, in the current version of the Acts, two of them, Peter and John, are represented as *ignorant and unlearned men:* and the opinion of some is, that this ignorance is similar to that, which, among ourselves, by its blunders and mistakes, so frequently disgraces the church and grieves the pious and judicious. Such an opinion, however, is a libel on their character, and a shameful impeachment of the wisdom which selected them. The passage, in the original, means that they were not chosen from the nobility, or the high stations in life; and that they had not received their education in the public seminaries of polite literature. They were at first selected from the whole number of disciples, and were carefully instructed for several years, by one " who taught as never man taught." Thus qualified, they did not need the wisdom of this world; nor did the gospel require it. The gospel is wretchedly perverted when it is made the channel of communication for the learning and the wisdom of men; its glory belongs to God, and not to men. Paul was a chosen vessel for this important purpose. For a time he might run mad with the spirit of persecution; might breathe out slaughter and death against the disciples: yet from his birth, in the design of heaven, he was selected and *separated unto the gospel.* While sitting at the feet of Gamaliel, he was acquiring that knowledge which rendered him an able minister of the New Testament. The wisdom of God endowed them, indeed, with miraculous powers, to meet the exigencies of that time. But miracles are never introduced to accomplish those purposes which can be answered in the ordinary way. The wisdom of God is manifested in selecting for the first preachers of the gospel, men of sound minds, capable of clear perceptions and correct decisions; men of accurate and extensive knowledge in all things pertaining to their office, who would not disgrace themselves and injure the cause they had espoused by the shameless blunders of ignorance; men of deep and fervent piety, who would preach, and live, and suffer, and die, for the glory of their Divine Master.

The death of Christ, and the preaching of the gospel could not be in vain. *He shall see of the travail of his soul; the word of God shall not re-*

turn to him void; it shall accomplish his pleasure. Millions of immortal souls shall be washed in the blood of the cross; changed and purified by that gospel proclaimed by the apostles and their successors. The salvation of each individual of all these countless millions, was a distinct and important object in the eternal purpose of God. In the great plan for promoting the divine glory is included a series of means, appointed and arranged by unerring wisdom, adapted to the character and circumstances of each individual. All, indeed, are saved by grace; but none are saved by miracle, or without the use of means. These means were not appointed and arranged by chance or by accident, neither of which, in the views and plans of God, have either meaning or existence: but with special design, to answer a particular purpose. Each series is a complete system in itself, embracing a number of parts, operating in perfect order and subordination to each other, all promoting the great object, the salvation of the soul. One part of these means, is to operate after another has produced its effect. One will have no good effect, until the mind has been first prepared by another. As the seasons of spring, summer, and autumn, by their united and successive influence, bring to maturity the fruits of the earth, so the different parts in each series of means, operate in building up the soul in its most holy faith. In its great outline, each series resembles all the others: but each one, in its details, is diversified by more than ten thousand peculiarities. Here we think, is a grand display of the wisdom—*the* MANIFOLD *wisdom of God.*

But lest we should be lost in so wide, though delightful a field, or wander through it with less advantage, let us take one single individual, and fix our attention on his case. This man is to be a vessel of mercy, is to be prepared to show forth the riches of divine glory. Let his birth be where it may; let his wanderings through the world be what they may; sooner or later, he must become acquainted with the gospel; for he cannot be saved without faith in Jesus Christ. He may fly from the command of God, like Jonah; but he will be overtaken and subdued. He may fight and persecute like Paul; but he will bless God for redeeming grace and sovereign mercy. He may too, like Paul, blaspheme; but he will embrace and cherish the faith which once he destroyed. He is surrounded by a series of means, arranged and set in operation before he was born, from which he cannot escape, by which, through divine agency, he is to become a new creature. Such is the case with every individual who shall, through the blood of the cross, reach the joys of heaven.

One object to be accomplished, in the salvation of a sinner is, to make him acquainted with the gospel; another is, by that gospel, to change his heart. In order that we may perceive the wisdom of God in adapting the means, and rendering them effectual to this purpose, we must consider the character on which the change is to be produced. The man who is to be the subject of this great work, is an intelligent creature; capable of perception, of thought, of reasoning, and of judgment; of course, though not an independent, yet he is a free agent.

The operations of his mind are free, and subject to no compulsion, except through the medium of perception. Perception is produced by impressions from external objects on the bodily senses, by statements made to the mind, and by its own exercise. These perceptions are the materials of thought; reasoning is the comparison of these thoughts with each other, and with a given standard; judgment, or decision, is the result of that comparison. The mind also possesses what are called moral powers. Its perceptions, thoughts, reasonings, and decisions, produce, in a greater or less degree, excitements of various kinds, or what are generally called affections or passions. These again have an important influence on the exercise of the intellectual faculties. They spread themselves, like an atmosphere, before the vision of the mind. They obscure or warp all its perceptions; of course affect, in a correspondent degree, all operations of the mind, depending on perception. Hence the most erroneous conclusions and incorrect decisions are made. Yet erroneous and incorrect as they are, they will excite their correspondent affections. These affections are the great motives of action; they direct the conduct. The man's life is the index to his affections, as his affections are to his thoughts and perceptions. In order to change his life, you must change his heart, or his affections; this can only be done by changing his thoughts and his conclusions; this again can be effected in no other way than by furnishing him with new materials of thought, by fixing attention, which is a strong effort of thought, on objects, in their nature calculated to produce this change. These materials of thought can be introduced in no other way than through the medium of perception; for that which does not enter the mind in this way can neither employ the thoughts, nor modify the affections.

This man is also a moral agent. He is capable of perceiving the nature and demands of a law, intended to regulate all his conduct, all his affections, and all his thoughts, and therefore called a moral law. God, his maker, has given him such a law, demanding, through his whole life, perfect conformity to its precepts in all his actions, affections, and thoughts. To such obedience the Great Lawgiver has promised the reward of his approbation, and threatens every transgression with his heavy displeasure. The transgression of this law is sin, and the liability to suffer its penalty is guilt. Now the man before us is a sinner, and is guilty. He, as all men are, is depraved. This depravity we will not at present attempt to define. Its nature and reality are illustrated and proved by numerous and melancholy facts, which meet the observation of all, and can be denied by none. All men have sinned; there is none righteous, no, not one. This man has transgressed this law; he does transgress it, not occasionally, but habitually; not accidentally, but designedly. The demands of this law are reasonable, its tendency is good; but there is not this belief in him: he believes these demands to be unreasonable, and this tendency to be inconsistent with his interest. He calculates on more happiness from transgression than from obedience. The law condemns him as a sinner, and threatens him with its penalty; he, therefore, hates this law with positive hatred. The character of God, in part, is made known through the law; he, therefore, hates that character, and the Being to whom it belongs. He loves sin, and neither intends nor desires to change his heart or his life. Hence it becomes his interest, as he conceives, to forget this law; and *God is not in all his thoughts;* he is *without God in the world.* For all his transgressions and hatred, there is not the shadow of excuse; nothing which he can plead in mitigation of his guilt. He is, therefore, in a state of just and fearful condemnation. Nor is it, by any efforts of his own, possible for him to escape, though he may forget this condemnation. The gospel offers him a way of escape, and invites him to accept of its provisions. But he rejects the offer, because he hates the provisions. He would accept of pardon, that is, exemption from punishment, if it was not connected with repentance. But this pardon is inseparably connected with repentance and reformation of heart and life. This pardon, therefore, he does not desire; all he desires is, permission to sin, to follow the inclination of his own heart with impunity. He loves those sins which repentance requires him to forsake; he has an utter aversion to the spirit which the gospel requires him to cherish, and to those duties, in the discharge of which he is to spend his future life. His deliberate and fixed intention is never to forsake these sins, never to cherish this spirit, never to discharge these duties. He may, as thousands have done, and as thousands are now doing, deceive himself with the supposition, that he intends, at some future period, to repent; but, in the nature of things, it is impossible. Such an intention cannot co-exist in the mind with a deliberate intention to live, at present, in sin. Light and darkness, Christ and Belial, might as soon dwell in harmony together, as two such intentions. To suppose it possible for a man to intend to repent in future, when at present he pursues and enjoys the pleasures of sin, is a dangerous delusion.

Such is the character that is to be changed. This life is to be reformed; this spirit is to be renewed; these affections are to be placed on heavenly and spiritual objects; these thoughts are to flow in a new channel; these perceptions are to be corrected.

In the accomplishment of this work, God manifests himself *mighty in strength and in wisdom.* Let us consider the means by which it is effected, and the manner in which they are employed.

The work is performed by the agency of the Holy Spirit; not in a miraculous way, but by the use of means, and chiefly by the instrumentality of truth. These means are, in themselves, wisely and powerfully calculated to have this effect. The gospel is the *power of God unto salvation to every one who believeth, the word of God is quick and powerful.* Indeed, the change is sometimes ascribed to the word: *Of his own will begat he us with the word of truth; being born again—of the word of God—the ingrafted word, which is able to save your souls.* Though it is effected by the use of means, it is as really the work of the Spirit, as if no means were employed. It is frequently ascribed to the Spirit without any reference to the means. Such is the ignorance of the mind, and the opposition of the heart, that these means would be effectually resisted, were they not accompanied by divine energy.

The sinner is commanded to believe and obey the gospel; but he feels an utter aversion to it, and disobeys the command. The Spirit does not, by compulsion, bring the mind instantly to submission; but in a way perfectly consistent with its free agency, brings it, step after step, to choose and delight in this submission. He will never change his life till his affections are changed. For it is not to be expected that he will voluntarily forsake those practices which all his affections prompt him to pursue. This would be inconsistent with the free agency of an intelligent mind. These affections are generated by his conclusions and his thoughts, and cannot be changed without first changing his thoughts; for in vain do you expect a change in the effect, while the cause of that effect is left, with undiminished vigour, in full operation. There is but one way, consistently with free agency, to change the thoughts; that is, by furnishing the mind with new materials of thought; with objects for their employment of the same nature with the affections which are to be excited. Control the thoughts, and you control the affections; control the affections, and you regulate the life. Suppose this order to be reversed, and if the same effect is produced, it must be by mere compulsion, by violating the free agency of man. But God, who has endowed him with this agency, will not destroy his own gift. This is the order which the wisdom of the Spirit observes in reforming the man: and there is an admirable adaptation to this order in the means by which the work is accomplished. This shows the great importance and necessity of truth, which, introduced into the mind, furnishes materials for the employment of its thoughts. The Spirit commences the work by fixing the attention on some truth relating to the nature of sin. This thoughtfulness is like leaven; its effects are immediately felt; it excites a correspondent degree of fear; this fear is the antagonist of the love of sin, and weakens the power of that love, and thus clears a little the vision of the mind, and opens the way for the entrance of other truths relating to the same subject. By the additional light of these truths, the thoughts are still more engaged, and the mind has clearer perceptions of the guilt and danger of sin; a greater degree of fear is excited; and, in the same proportion, the love of sin loses its power. One truth opens the way for another; and the more intensely the attention dwells on the subject, the more deeply interesting does it become. The sinner is now perplexed and alarmed with the view of his guilt and danger. This prompts to further inquiries, and the result of these inquiries increases his alarm. His views and feelings with regard to sin are changed. Instead of the fond, though delusive dreams and hopes of impunity, the danger of sin now fills his mind and occupies his thoughts; instead of the love, the fear of sin and its consequences now prevail; instead of a desire for the pleasure of sin, he now feels anxious and distressed on account of it. He is not, in the scriptural sense, a new man, yet he is another from what he formerly was. This is conviction for sin; that is, the perception and belief of the truth respecting it.

Universal experience, if we are not mistaken, will testify that this is the way in which the work of grace commences: with serious thoughtfulness. It is a fact too, that the more we attend to any subject the better we understand it. The truth which engaged the first thought, may have been presented to the mind before, but did not, in the same degree, arrest the attention: this, then, is the work of the Spirit, whose design it was, in this way, to produce that deep thoughtfulness, and that sense of danger, which we now perceive. When the man bestowed the first thought on the subject, he had no intention or desire of proceeding so far: this, however, was the intention of the Spirit. Had he been commanded, before the seriousness commenced, to give up the world and cease thinking about it, he would have disobeyed; but now the world has slipped out of his mind and is forgotten, in proportion as his thoughts are otherwise employed. In vain would the command have been given, in his former days—think of the Saviour; inquire after the plan of salvation; seek a remedy for sin: but now the inquiry is naturally and earnestly made, *What must I do to be saved?* Having clearer discoveries of the deceitfulness and wickedness of his own heart; thoroughly convinced that he deserves condemnation, that he is utterly unable to deliver himself; he believes and feels that if he is saved, it must be by the exercise of mercy; mercy too, which he does not deserve, and which he cannot demand; for God is not bound to save him. No man can be reconciled to the everlasting displeasure of God, who has any correct ideas of that displeasure. He now sees, however, that he cannot escape, except it is by an act of sovereign grace. He is now completely subdued. His thoughts are turned to this mercy, which promises the only safety; for this mercy, with humble, submissive earnestness he prays. The Holy Spirit, who directs this progress, fixes his attention on the promises and invitations of the gospel, which are now most deeply interesting to him, and through which the Saviour and the mercy of God are offered. He is now willing to be saved in any way which God is pleased to appoint. While meditating on these subjects, he is enabled to have a spiritual discernment of the promises and invitations of the gospel; he sees the suitableness of Jesus Christ as a Saviour, to his sinful and helpless condition; he feels a movement of his whole soul towards this Saviour; clearer views of the plan of salvation increase this movement; he believes, he adores, he loves, he hopes, he rejoices, he weeps, he gives himself up without reserve to God and to his Redeemer. He is now, in the scriptural sense, a new man. His thoughts have been employed about the truth of the Bible; his affections are changed with his thoughts; and his life will change with his affections. The purity of God and of his law, to which he felt such a deep-rooted enmity, is now most lovely in his view; the service of God, to which he felt so much aversion, is now his delight. The Saviour, of whom he thought so seldom before, and whom he so lightly esteemed, now fills his mind, and is precious to his heart; the Bible, formerly, in his estimation without interest and much neglected, or at best nothing more than a dead letter, is now life, and spirit, and power, and employs his meditations day and night; the world, formerly so enchanting in his eye, which he loved so dearly and pursued so eagerly, is now stripped of its delusive charms, sinks to its proper place in his regard, and commands him no more. In heaven he lays up his treasure, and views it as the blessed and glorious state where he will spend his eternal existence.

Behold the wisdom manifested in this change! It displays design, as clearly as design can be displayed; not of the man, but of the Spirit who commenced and accomplished the work; a design which unfolds itself, more and more completely, at each progressive stage of the process. There is a decisive control exercised over his thoughts and affections, and yet he is conscious of no control. Every step is voluntarily taken, with as much freedom as it could have been, if no such control had been employed. To the first truth which occupied his thoughts, he felt no very decided opposition; because he was not aware of the consequence, did not perceive nor suspect its connection with the result. Had he been assured that this truth was connected with another, and this again with another, forming a complete system of means intended to bring him to believe and obey the gospel, his opposition would have been roused, and would have resisted the entrance of that truth into his mind. The first truth was, however, admitted, without awakening any hostile suspicion, to employ his thoughts; this opened the way for the second, with which it was connected; this, for the third; and this, for the fourth, and so on; until he dwells with inquisitive earnestness and delight on the promises which encourage the guilty and helpless sinner to hope for pardon. One part of the means is to operate on the mind in that state in which another leaves it; and this again leaves it in a state of preparation for another. There is a connection, an order and subserviency in the means, admirably adapted to the manner in which the mind is to be influenced and changed. Truth flows into his mind in answer to his own desires and inquiries; and by this truth the Spirit unfolds his designs, and carries on his work. The man now, from choice, hates and forsakes the very sins which he once loved and pursued; now delights in those devotional exercises of the heart, and in those religious duties which he formerly hated and neglected. In the day of divine power, he is a willing subject of grace. All this is true of every Christian: for each one of them there is a system of means, thus wisely arranged, and thus effectually applied.

Now, if it be a fact, that exhibitions of wisdom do improve the understanding which contemplates and labours to comprehend them, then every Christian has such an opportunity of improving in considering the means by which his own heart was changed, and the manner in which that change was effected. The work may not, in every one, have progressed with a regularity which, in all its stages, and all its minute details, will accord with the above statement; but will, we conceive, be substantially the same. Nor is it a subject on which he can ever feel indifferent: it will always be interesting to him. Often will he review the whole process, from the commencement to the present hour, for it is a work which will continue through life. He can dwell with thoughtful inspection on each step separately, and in connection with every other. His mind may not be enlightened by science, but he will have, in his own heart, the means of improving his understanding, by attentively and frequently beholding a display of divine wisdom which the material universe cannot surpass.

SECTION III.

Exhibitions of Greatness improve the Understanding.

EXPERIENCE teaches us that the contemplation of *greatness* strengthens and improves the understanding. The mind is conscious of an effort to grasp the magnitude, the vastness of the object, or the scene which it views. A pleasing expansion is the consequence of these efforts. This is the true feeling of the sublime. The mind seems to be endowed with some degree of that greatness which it beholds. Now, in this respect the Christian system has very far the advantage over the whole universe of matter. In considering the material creation, there is a limit beyond which the mind cannot, with any profit, carry its investigations; such efforts are repaid with neither pleasure nor improvement to the mind that makes them. There is no more known, at this day, respecting the principle of attraction, than was known at the end of Newton's life. The distance, the diameter, and the different periods of the planets, are already ascertained: inquiry, therefore, on these subjects has ceased. And subjects on which nothing more can be known, yield little or no improvement. For it is not so much the possession, as the acquisition of ideas that improves the mind. Memory alone is exercised in retaining our ideas; but the understanding is exercised, and of course improved in their acquisition. Besides, the grandest scenes of nature cease to be interesting, as soon as they become familiar to the mind. Those who live on the summit of a mountain, derive not one pleasing emotion from beholding that prospect which fills the mind of a stranger with inexpressible delight, and gives it a conscious elevation. Those who view the restless ocean every day, cease to admire its boundless extent; but on the man who views it for the first time, it has a very different effect. From our infancy we are accustomed to see the sun, shining in all his majesty, rising and setting regularly every day; we see the moon and stars pursuing their nightly procession; but there is no novelty in the scene: their appearance one day and one night is so nearly the same with every other day and night, that no attention is excited. Could we rise, with our present faculties of mind and body, from the centre of the earth, language could not express the sublime feelings which the first view of the lofty concave, either by night or by day, would not fail to produce. The case is widely different with moral greatness: here, there is no limit to check further inquiries and further progress. Nor is it possible to exhaust subjects of this nature so completely, that nothing new will remain to invite and repay progressive investigation. The discoveries in natural science may be communicated to others, who know neither the toil nor the pleasure of that inquiry which led to them; but our progress in the knowledge of God, through the cross, must be the result of our own efforts, and our own experience. One may assist in directing the inquiries of another, but cannot relieve him from the necessity of making these inquiries; they must be made by each individual for himself. Language cannot impart to another the views and feelings which reward the diligent student of moral greatness. One cannot commence his progress where that of another has ended; each one commences from the same point.

The Apostle Paul prays that the Ephesians might *know the love of Christ;* and yet, in the very next words declares that this love *passeth knowledge.* Here is neither paradox nor inconsistency. This love is infinite; and therefore, never can be perfectly known by any creature. Its height, no limited mind can reach; its depth, none can fathom; its length and its breadth, none can comprehend. Yet the Christian who devoutly meditates on this subject will be rewarded, every day and every year, with such proficiency as will increase his strength, and his desire, to persevere the next day, and the next year, in the contemplation of redeeming love. Not an effort is made, not a day is spent, in vain.

The progress he makes does not damp his ardour, and diminish his joy, by the conviction that the less remains to be done. The further he advances, the wider does the range of future progress expand on his view. The higher he rises, the more sublime does the height appear which he has yet to reach. Nor is it possible for any length of time to render the subject so familiar to his mind, that it will cease to arrest his attention, and invite him to further pursuit. Every step he advances, every degree he rises, presents him with increasing wonders more inviting and more delightful, than all he has yet known. All behind him, and all below him is forgotten, in view of what is still before him and above him. No attainment, no progress satisfies him, while so much remains unattained. The brightest visions of faith and hope can present to his mind nothing more enrapturing, than to spend his eternal existence in knowing more and more of the love of Christ.

There is a greatness in the mercy of God, which no finite understanding can ever comprehend; which yet rewards the mind engaged in the contemplation of it, with the purest delight and the most encouraging success. *For as the heaven is high above the earth, so great is his mercy toward them that fear them.* Let us, for a moment, attend to this comparison. Nothing in the material universe conveys more forcibly to the mind the idea and the impression of greatness, than the heaven.

Its lofty height, its vast extent, are calculated to produce impressions truly sublime. A single glance will produce the conviction that no human effort can ever reach it. With all the aid which art can afford, the greatest elevation to which man can ascend from this earth, does not appear to diminish, in the smallest degree, the height of heaven. Although we cannot say, with strict propriety, that its height appears to be infinite; yet, certainly, it is very great. This height, then, above the earth, is the scale by which we should measure the greatness of redeeming mercy.

In language by no means of dubious import, we sometimes hear threatening hints, that the progress of modern science will, one day, shake the foundation and overthrow the whole system of Christianity; that man will become too wise to believe that there is any such thing as sin, in this poor miserable world; of course, that there is no need of the mercy of God, or of a Saviour. We rejoice, most cordially, in the progress of science; and cannot, for a moment, be made to fear such effects from that progress. The Bible was not intended to teach us the science of nature; its object is infinitely more important. We cannot believe, however, that the greatest proficient in this science will find a single fact, or make a single discovery at variance with the truth of this Holy Book. If Christianity needed such aid, the light of true philosophy would furnish it, in abundance. Such, at least, is the fact respecting the passage now under consideration. Modern astronomers assure us that the canopy over our heads is not real substance, coloured with soft and cheerful blue, along the surface of which, the sun, the moon and the stars, pursue their daily and nightly courses; that if we should take our flight to the remotest star which our eye can perceive, and pursue our flight in the same direction as far beyond that star as it is from the earth; and repeat this flight ten thousand times, till the whole system to which we belong should vanish out of sight, still numerous other systems, like our own, should alternately swell on our view, and then disappear; the same appearance of the sky would accompany us as we advanced, and surround us when we stopped; that no real substance would ever check our flight; that the impression made on our senses is produced by infinite space. This, then, is the measure of divine mercy; it is not only very great; it is literally boundless, it is infinite mercy.

The greatness of this adorable perfection may be perceived by considering the amount of guilt which it washes away, the multitude of sins which it covers. This is a subject too, which very often and very deeply engages the attention of every Christian. He must be often employed in meditating on the number of his transgressions, and on the circumstances which aggravate his guilt; these he confesses before God; on account of these he is humbled; for these he repents, and implores forgiveness. Let him be ignorant of what else he may, if a Christian, he cannot be ignorant of his own sinfulness. Nor can he cherish the hope of pardon without perceiving the greatness of that mercy on which his hopes are founded. Take one day in the life of a man unrenewed by divine grace; calculate, if possible, the number of thoughts, desires, and intentions, the words and actions of this one day; all of which are sinful; each one of which deserves the displeasure of God; and under what a load of guilt will he not repose himself at night? And yet he wakes, and pursues the same course for another day. Multiply this number by three hundred and sixty-five, and it will give you the number of sins, and the amount of guilt for one year. What a treasure is this, which he has laid up, not of silver and gold, but of wrath! And yet he commences another year with the same intention. This guilt is not to be ascertained, however, by the mere simple ratio of multiplication; but by a compound ratio of increase. Every day is more guilty than the one which precedes it. Every day the calls to repentance are louder and louder; every day his danger is more and more alarming. He cannot, therefore, persevere in these circumstances without a degree of guilt, increasing as the motives to repentance become more impressive and urgent. Besides, his thirst for sin is increased with the indulgence of every day; so is the rapidity with which he is carried along the broad

road to ruin. Like a body falling to the earth, the nearer he approaches the pit of perdition, he is drawn towards it with an increasing velocity. Such is one day; and such is one year! Suppose he remains in this state for twenty years, every day, and hour, and moment of which is spent in sin. Then multiply the product of one year by twenty, and it will give (what our minds cannot possibly comprehend) the number of sins with all their aggravations, which are freely pardoned through the mercy of God, when he is united to Christ and adopted into the family of heaven. Every sinner who lays hold of this hope, is convinced that if God was not *rich in mercy*, his sins could not be forgiven. Nor can he ever become indifferent to the greatness of this mercy. Every thought which he casts back on his past sinfulness, every pulse of spiritual life which beats in his heart, every ray of hope which cheers and rejoices his soul, forcibly remind him of it. There is, in this greatness, an interesting and infinite loveliness, which invites and engages his attention, and fills him with a pure and peaceful joy. His earnest prayer is, that, with a tongue faltering in death, he may recommend this ground of hope to those he leaves behind; that when at the call of his Saviour, he is removed from this earth, his thoughts and his hopes may be firmly fixed on the greatness of divine mercy.

It may be thought unnecessary and useless to search for additional evidence of the greatness of sovereign mercy, when that already presented, in the salvation of one sinner, places the subject so far above our comprehension.

The Christian, however, cannot be wearied with the subject; he loves to meditate on it; to view it in all the grandeur and sublimity of its exhibitions; to feel overwhelmed with its incomprehensibilities; because he is the more deeply convinced that it is calculated to afford him an eternal *fulness of joy*. This Christian is not the only *vessel of mercy*, the only monument of its greatness. Countless millions will be redeemed through this mercy; each one of whom will display the riches of its glory. If the utmost power of numbers could answer the purpose, and if our minds could perform the operation of multiplying all these millions by the greatness of mercy displayed in the salvation of one sinner, the result would not exceed the truth, however it might exceed our comprehension. But numbers have no relation to this subject; our minds cannot perform the operation. It is a subject, known and comprehended by Him alone, to whose character this perfection belongs. The Christian can feel no regret that the foundation of his hope is so deep and firm that he cannot comprehend it; that the source of his joy is as inexhaustible as the infinite mind in which it exists. It would grieve him to believe that there was a period, however remote, in his future existence, when the last mysteries of this greatness would be completely developed to his view; when nothing remained to invite further inquiries, and promise new discoveries; when the whole subject would become familiar to his mind. With painful anticipations he would look forward to such a period, as the termination of at least a part of his joy. It will expand and elevate the mind of the highest archangel to behold the great multitude redeemed out of every tongue and kindred under heaven; a multitude, requiring of this angel, perhaps the flight of an age, to take a survey of all their crowded millions, presenting to his consideration the same general features of character, connected, however, with infinite varieties and shades of difference. This exhibition of divine mercy may fix him more firmly in his allegiance to the great Jehovah. Thus the thrones, and dominions, and principalities and powers of heaven will be reconciled to God, through the cross of Christ. Deriving more exalted conceptions of the divine character from these exhibitions, their love will glow with more intense ardour, their adoration will be more profound, their songs of praise will be louder and sweeter. While the universe is filled with the splendours of mercy, reflected from the saints of the Most High, the divine Saviour will rejoice over them as the purchase of his blood, as the fruit of his agonies on the cross. With ineffable complacency, God himself will view them as the most precious jewels in his crown of glory.

There is a greatness in the forbearance of God,

which, however it may pass unnoticed by a thoughtless world, cannot fail to employ the meditations of the Christian. Through this forbearance he escapes, from day to day, the punishment his crimes deserve. There is this peculiarity in the long-suffering of God; it is exercised towards every human being. If there be a truth, supported by the testimony of Scripture and of fact, it is this; that man, from his very birth, is in a state of guilt. In many places the Bible, in plain and positive language, declares this truth. We feel in ourselves, and we witness in others, nameless sufferings, for which no satisfactory account can be given, but that we are guilty; and that these sufferings are the consequence of this guilt. It is evident, at the same time, that these sufferings are not proportioned to our guilt; of course, that they are intended to operate as means of reformation. Every sin deserves a far greater punishment than is ever inflicted in this life. Every moment, therefore, that we are permitted to remain in a state of rebellion, on this earth, displays the greatness of the divine forbearance. This will be, to the Christian, a cause of grateful adoration through his eternal existence; and the sinner who perishes in final impenitence, sinking and suffering in the bottomless pit, will remember, with anguish, that once the long-suffering of God waited with him.

Although God is the self-existent, eternal Jehovah, and we are creatures of yesterday, sinful worms of the earth, yet he permits us to aid our conceptions of his greatness by comparison. Let us then suppose an earthly sovereign, distinguished for the mildness and equity of his laws, and for the wisdom and benevolence with which he labours to guard and promote the happiness of his subjects : and that a part of these subjects rebel against him, traduce his character, disobey his laws, and endeavour, by their example and their advice, to lead others into the same rebellion, destroy the government, and fill the whole province with discord, anarchy, and ruin. He has it completely in his power to crush them, at any moment ; and is well acquainted with their designs and their efforts. From pure benevolence, he labours to soften and subdue them by kindness ; and, therefore, offers them pardon, invites them to return to the protection of his government, and to the enjoyment of his approbation—the rich reward of all faithful subjects. Messenger after messenger is sent to offer this pardon, to urge them with earnest entreaties to accept of it, and warn them of their danger. But they reject the offer, make light of the warning, and grow bolder in rebellion. Again, perhaps at the peril of their lives, the messengers return to them, with more earnest entreaties, and more solemn and affectionate warnings. But the tenderness and urgency with which the offers are made and the warnings are given, increase their dislike into hatred of his character, his government, and his offers. Again they are visited : and their hatred is matured into deep-rooted enmity, and defiance begins to print itself on their brow. How long would this sovereign bear with such treatment from such rebels? How soon would his patience be exhausted, his clemency turned into just indignation, and his power be exerted in their destruction? How striking, then, how glorious is the patience of God, who bears with the rebellion, the wickedness, the enmity, the insulting blasphemy of man, from day to day, from year to year, and from age to age! When the deadly, the infernal malignity of sin; when the infinite mercy and majesty of God, against whom it was committed, are seen in the light of eternity, the greatness of the divine forbearance will touch the heart of men and angels with sentiments of the most profound and joyful adoration.

Now, it is impossible for any one to be a Christian without being sensible of the exceeding greatness of the divine patience towards him. Nothing can efface from his mind the remembrance of his former sinfulness and his guilt. The vileness and malignity of his sins he will often confess and lament before God; and the divine forbearance which waited with him, is so necessarily connected with sin, that the remembrance and impression of the one will introduce the other. To remember his sins, and forget the long-suffering of God, will be impossible; the greatness of which will be graduated, in his view, by the amount of his guilt. With the most intense thoughtfulness he will often review his past offences, the dangers to which he was exposed, the perilous escapes he has made, till he finds himself instinctively, though imperceptibly shrinking, as if he was at the moment exposed to the same danger. He will be filled with wonder and amazement that he was not stricken dead in the midst of his sins; that the patience of God could bear with such a provoking and daring offender. These emotions are the necessary consequence of his utter inability, after all his efforts, to comprehend the greatness of his forbearance. The vileness of sin, and the amount of his guilt, will increase, in his view, with every advance he makes in the divine life, with every degree by which he draws nearer to God; and in the same proportion will this greatness rise and expand above and beyond his comprehension.

There is, indeed, a greatness, an infinite greatness belonging to all the perfections of Deity; to his power, his knowledge, his justice, &c., as well as to his wisdom, his mercy, and his forbearance. On this greatness, the Christian will often meditate with deep interest and delight. His thoughts, his admiration, his love, his adoration of the greatness of these perfections, displayed in the works of creation, of providence, and redemption, will constitute the high and holy intercourse which he is permitted to hold, here on earth, with God his Maker; and in this way he will *see* and *enjoy God*, as his portion, when finally released from the darkness and imperfections of the present state, and raised to the clearer light and vision of eternity.

Let us now briefly review the subject. The proposition, for the illustration of which these remarks are offered, is: That the Bible has a direct and powerful tendency to improve the understanding of those who study its historical narratives, its doctrines and its precepts ; but more especially, that it will invigorate with increasing strength the understanding of the true Christian, who is deeply interested in securing the salvation of his soul ; with whom religion is not a mere name, an empty profession ; not a mere collection of ideas, or a system of external ceremonies, neither of which have any practical effect on his heart or his life ; but an important reality, such a knowledge and belief of the truth as calls into vigorous exertion all the powers of the understanding and the heart. If the proposition and the remarks with which it is accompanied are true, the inference will be that the mind of the Christian is more improved than the mind of any other man. We do not shrink from this inference, but admit it, as fair and necessary, which the preceding observations are intended to support. These observations derive their pertinency and their force from this principle : that whatever calls into vigorous exercise the intellectual faculties, will improve these faculties ; and that the improvement will be in proportion to the variety, the complex nature, and the magnitude of the objects about which the mind is employed. This, it is universally admitted, is the effect resulting from literary pursuits. Take two youths, of equal capacity and strength of mind; let one of them spend eight or ten years, while his mind is unfolding and his intellectual character is forming, in the study of languages and science; let the other spend the same time engaged in some of the ordinary occupations of life; at the end of this period, which of them would be best qualified for investigation, for correct discrimination and decision? Which of them would make the greatest proficiency in the study of law, of medicine, or theology? The student undoubtedly would have the advantage over the other: not so much on account of the ideas with which his mind is stored: but chiefly on account of the discipline through which his mind has passed, and the habits of investigating, of reasoning, and of judging which he has acquired. The conclusion, therefore, is just and unavoidable, that on the same principle, according to the preceding remarks, the religion of the Bible will improve the mind which cordially embraces it.

Nor do we fear the result of a comparison between the Christian and any other man, provided the comparison be a fair one. Let both, in all other respects, be equal; let the only difference be, that one is a man of scriptural piety, of experimental religion, and the other is not, and we hesitate not to affirm that the comparison will result in favour of the Christian, and in support of our conclusion. We know, indeed, that comparisons may be made which would furnish a very different result. With a Christian of moderate talents, doomed to labour from day to day, to gain a scanty subsistence, who knows but little more than his Bible and his God—you may compare a man of the world, or even a professed infidel, possessing a native vigour of mind, cultivated by study, embellished with science; and suppose that the result of this comparison will overthrow our conclusion. While you make this comparison, however, candour will compel you to acknowledge that it is not a fair one. Let the Christian possess the same native vigour of mind, enjoy the same literary advantages, with the man of the world; or let the irreligious man possess the same moderate talents, be engaged in the same daily toils, be denied, in the same degree, all opportunities of mental improvement, with the Christian; then the result will triumphantly support our conclusion. In the former case the result is derived from other circumstances, in which the man of the world has greatly the advantage; in the latter, in all respects except religion, they are equal; and the result is derived solely from the difference made by the influence of the spirit and the truth of God. With sorrow it must be admitted, too, that thousands who profess the religion of Jesus Christ are nothing but mere pretenders, uninfluenced by its renovating spirit and its power. Such are not, and cannot be, examples of the various and happy effects produced by the influence of the Bible. No cause will produce its effects where it does not exist, and where it does not operate. The zealous advocate for literary studies would complain, and justly too, if the tendency of these studies was tried by the example of those, who, though they had spent the usual time in academies and colleges, were known to be nothing but mere pretenders to literary acquisitions. He would point you to the man who loved the pursuits in which he was engaged, whose mind was closely and habitually applied to these studies, as the example which would illustrate and support his proposition. *Go thou and do likewise*, with the principles of the Bible; look for their effects, where they are in actual and vigorous operation.

It is readily admitted that among the Greeks and Romans, who were ignorant of divine revelation, there were many whose minds were improved with the knowledge of arts and sciences, in a degree far above thousands of Christians. This admission, however, does not in the least affect our conclusion. No man will affirm that their minds could not have been improved in a greater degree than they were, by the application of means calculated to produce this effect. We contend that the Bible furnishes these very means; that the knowledge and belief of its truth would have improved their minds in a still greater degree, and have rendered them still more illustrious than they are. If Archimedes had been a sincere, an humble, and devout Christian, he might have been the Newton of the world. If Socrates, Plato, Aristotle, and Seneca had felt the transforming light and power of the Book of God, they might have filled the place now occupied by Locke, and Reid, and Beattie, and Paley.

PART II.

SECTION I.

Economy and Industry, taught in the Bible—promote human Happiness.

According to the design with which these remarks were commenced, it remains to point out the powerful and happy tendency of the Bible in reforming the moral character of man,—and thus to save him, in a great degree, from the miseries of this life; and to furnish him the best consolation and support under those from which he cannot escape. To improve the heart, indeed, is the purpose for which the Bible is professedly given: its fitness to answer this purpose declares the wisdom and goodness of its divine Author. Many of the afflictions which man is doomed to suffer in this life, are the necessary and immediate result of his own folly, imprudence, and wickedness; of his wilful neglect of the lessons taught him in the Bible, and his persevering disobedience to its precepts. From all these miseries, those who understand, believe, and obey this holy book, will be preserved.

It is obvious that man requires a daily sustenance, adapted to his animal nature, and that this sustenance is to be provided by his own labour. Economy, in the management and use of the fruit of this labour, is therefore a duty which we owe to ourselves, to each other, and to God. We have no rules laid down in systematic order on this subject: yet we have the words of our Saviour, which, taken in connection with the occasion on which they were spoken, will furnish a complete, though compendious system of economy—*Gather up the fragments that remain, that nothing be lost.* Here was no immediate want, for all were satisfied; yet this is no excuse for criminal waste. The disciples might have supposed, after witnessing this astonishing miracle, that the broken pieces which were left were not worthy of any care. He teaches them, however, a different lesson; these fragments are to be carefully preserved for future occasions.. Was the spirit of this example and this precept in full operation, it would prevent a very great amount of perplexity and suffering. There are thousands who, with economy, might enjoy all the real comforts of life, and fill a respectable station in society; and yet by wastefulness and inattention to small matters, soon find their resources insufficient for their wants. A debt is contracted to supply the present deficiency. The same want of economy prevails, and prevents the acquisition of means to discharge, at the proper time, this debt. Another debt, however, is contracted to discharge the first, and to supply another deficiency, arising out of the same wasteful habit. Though without economy, they are not yet, perhaps without credit; another debt of still larger amount is contracted. Credit at length begins to fail; and payment is more and more urgently solicited, but cannot be conveniently made. Perplexities beginning to thicken around them, some other expedient must be tried; but not the expedient of economy and self-denial. There is a prospect of speculation, which may have a fortunate issue; prizes of large amount are floating in the lottery wheel; a ticket will not cost much, and it *may* draw a prize. The speculation however fails; the ticket comes out a blank. The amount of debt is increased by the means intended to discharge it. Creditors become more urgent; the civil officer is employed; property is sold, and the debts are not paid. Perplexity ripens into trouble; the terrible oath of insolvency is taken. Ways and means are suggested, and too often pursued, not consistent with strict honesty, but which, it is thought, necessity demands, and will, *perhaps*, justify. Their independence, their standing in society, and in some degree their regard to character, are lost; strong inducements to correct deportment are withdrawn; the door to injustice, fraud, and vice is opened, and too often entered; and trouble matures into actual misery. We would not affirm that in every case, all this is the consequence of wastefulness alone; other causes, as will presently appear, may co-operate in commencing and hastening this progress to ruin and distress. Observation, however, will justify the conclusion, that much of it might be prevented by habits of economy, by gathering up the fragments, and taking care that nothing be lost.

Small matters are neglected and suffered to waste, merely because they are small. Separately considered, their value may be but little; yet collectively, they will amount to something of consequence. The fragments which our Saviour directed to be gathered up, were small broken pieces, separately of little value; but when collected, they filled *twelve baskets*—a very important provision for future want. If our resources be scanty, economy will enable us to derive from them the greatest degree of comfort which they can yield; if they be ample, by gathering up the fragments, we will be enabled to do so much the more good, and to taste so much the more of that blessedness which arises from giving, from preventing, or relieving the sufferings of others. The man, whose moderate income is no more than sufficient for his own support, by economy, will derive more real enjoyment from that income, and will maintain his independence, so dear to every human heart; and this noble independence will increase his influence, his respectability and usefulness in society. The man of more affluent circumstances, by exercising economy in the provisions of his table, in the expense of his furniture and his dress, without diminishing his rational comfort in the least, might increase the means of doing good, and elevate himself in the estimation of others. That man is mistaken who expects his respectability and influence to be in proportion to the sumptuous provisions of his table, and the expensiveness of his dress and his furniture. The epicure will admire his table, to which he will be drawn by all the power of appetite, and thousands will admire the elegance of his dress and his equipage. But what kind of feeling is this, and of what real value is it in the view of well-improved minds? That of the epicure is merely an animal feeling, and has no regard to either intellectual or moral excellence as its object; that of others is evanescent, and if it has any object among human beings, it is not the proprietor, but the artist by whom the articles which excite these feelings were made.

Moral excellence is the object of the most valuable and the most desirable feelings of the human heart: this alone renders a man truly respectable and beloved by others. Active and persevering beneficence gives rise to that influence, and calls forth those affections most desirable to a good and a wise man. To such a man the blessing of those who were ready to perish is a thousand times more grateful than all the admiration wealth ever produced. Look at the man whose influence depends on his wealth; you will see him surrounded with multitudes who admire the glitter which affluence throws around him, and with other multitudes of obsequious and cringing dependents. But the man is no sooner in his grave than all this feeling is transferred to his successor; for wealth, and not moral excellence, is its object. Compare with this man the benevolent Howard, whose path was through the prison and the dungeon—whose home was with the friendless and distressed—the very fragments of whose fortune were preserved and devoted to the relief of human misery. The influence of Howard remains indicated by that warmth of approbation with which the heart is drawn towards him. Posterity will feel and acknowledge the lasting influence of that pure and active benevolence with which his life was distinguished. Take the lady around whom wealth has shed its most fascinating splendours; compare the feelings associated with her name, with those which are strongly associated with the name of Isabella Graham. The name of the one awakens the remembrance of the sumptuous collation, the tumult of the merry dance, the gaieties of the splendid drawing-room: the name of the other is associated with labours of love, with tears of sorrow wiped away, with the widow's heart singing for joy, with destitute orphans, clothed, instructed, and cherished with maternal tenderness. Which of these would you rather be, in the estimation and feelings of posterity? which of them, in the view of our omniscient Judge? Without economy, neither Howard nor Mrs. Graham could have done as much good as they actually have done; and it is by the good they have done they live in our hearts, and will continue to live in the hearts of unborn generations; when the name of those who squandered their wealth on mere animal gratifications, on the gaieties of life, shall be forgotten. When mere animal appetite is to be gratified, the table of the rich is welcome; when literary taste seeks for pleasure, the productions of genius are valued; but when sorrow and distress are to be relieved, when the wounded spirit is to be healed, the bleeding heart to be soothed and comforted, we naturally look to the man of economical habits, of benevolent dispositions, of tender and compassionate feelings. How strong and how endearing, then, should be our attachment to Jesus Christ, the friend of the helpless, the Saviour of sinners; and how unbounded the influence with which he should reign over our hearts and our lives!

A vast amount of human misery may be traced to idleness, all which would be prevented by preventing the idleness from which it flows. Those who observe the Bible as their rule of life will be preserved from this vicious habit, which, in that holy volume, is most explicitly reprobated, and its tendency to misery clearly pointed out.

An idle soul shall suffer hunger: That ye study to be quiet, and to do your own business, and to work with your own hands, as we commanded you; that ye may walk honestly toward them that are without, and that ye may have lack of nothing. From these and other passages which might be quoted, it appears that want, pinching want, is the consequence of idleness; and our own observation confirms the remark. The manna no longer falls from the clouds, nor does the earth yield her increase without the labour of man. His wants cannot be supplied without his own industry, nor can his appetite be long denied. Hence a state of want opens the door to vice of the most atrocious character. The prayer of Agur is as wise as it is pious—*Remove far from me—poverty: lest I be poor and steal, and take the name of my God in vain.* That man whose moral principle does not restrain him from idleness, will probably not hesitate to steal, or resort to some dishonest method of procuring his daily subsistence. The next step will be, in order to escape suspicion and detection, to take the name of God in vain, either in false and profane asseverations of his innocence, or in actual perjury. He will not, however, be believed; he cannot live without the supplies which nature requires; if these are not provided by honest industry, they must be obtained in some other way. His idleness, therefore, will be a much stronger proof of his guilt, than his profane and positive declarations, or even his perjury, can be of his innocence. Sooner or later, he will be detected, and detection will be followed by punishment and disgrace. If none but the worthless idler himself was involved, the case would not be so distressing; but his family and his relatives are heirs to some degree of his misery and disgrace, and especially if among these there should be a pious heart, that heart will feel an anguish not surpassed by the piercing of a thousand daggers.

The human mind is naturally active, and will be employed; if not engaged in some regular and useful occupation, it will be employed in disturbing the peace of society. *Withal*, says Paul, speaking of certain characters, *they learn to be idle, wandering about from house to house; and not only idle, but tattlers also, and busy-bodies, speaking things which they ought not.* Paul was a philosopher, as well as an inspired writer. Tell him the nature of a cause, and he will tell you the effects which will result from its operation. Tell him that a woman (and it is of women he is here speaking) is neither employed in *looking well to the ways of her household*, nor in works of charity, nor in religious duties, but is idle; he will tell you, that if she is not led from a sense of duty to a life of industry, she will have no resources within herself to furnish the mind with pleasing employment, she will seek a refuge from the barrenness and solitude of her own vacant mind in the company of others; that as the company of such a person can neither be very useful nor agreeable, she will not be pressed to make long visits; she will therefore go from house to house; but as she wishes to appear of some consequence, and that her visits may appear to have some object, she will necessarily become a *tattler*; she will overflow with trifling, impertinent and mischievous conversation; and in order to collect abundant materials for this ceaseless *tale-bearing*, she will next become a busy-body, impertinently meddling with the concerns of others, officiously offering her advice, insidiously tempting them to an unreserved expression of their opinion; with eagerness she will catch what they say; and what they do not say, she will supply from suspicion and conjecture: dressing up the whole with her own exaggeration, misrepresentation, and colouring, she will fly from house to house, the herald of scandal, and the harbinger of strife and contention. Who has not witnessed the peace of families disturbed, whole neighbourhoods embroiled in discord and cruel animosities which terminate, perhaps, only with life, by the mischievous prattling of one such tale-bearer? Her idleness and her officious meddling, her empty, perhaps malicious loquacity, will soon recoil, with fearful effect, upon herself. When her character is known, her presence will impose a restraint on that free and unreserved conversation, which is the life of friendship, and which might flow with safety into bosoms under the restraint of religious principle. She will be the terror of society; and her visits will be dreaded by all families who wish to live in peace and harmony. *One sinner destroyeth much good.* Contrasted with such an one, how *blessed is the peace maker.*

Compare with this tattler, the character of the virtuous woman, given in the 30th chapter of Proverbs. The one has lost the confidence and affection of all; the other is highly esteemed and beloved—for *her price is above rubies;* especially does the heart of her husband, who knows her best, repose in her with perfect safety. The one is idle, *working not at all;* the other *looketh well to the ways of her household, and eateth not the bread of idleness;* she provides clothing for her family, and they *are not afraid of the snow.* Nor is it an excuse for idleness that her own family are abundantly supplied; she has other important objects to answer with the fruit of her industry; *she maketh fine linen and selleth it, and delivereth girdles to the merchant.* Thus she is provided with the means of doing good and relieving the sufferings of others; *she stretcheth out her hand to the poor; yea, she reacheth forth her hands to the needy.* The tattler is wandering about, *speaking things which she ought not,* with an untamed, unbridled *tongue, full of deadly poison, setting on fire the course of nature;* the virtuous woman *openeth her mouth with wisdom; and in her tongue is the law of kindness.* How wide is the difference, perceived from this contrast! The one is idle, wandering about tattling, impertinently meddling, retailing scandal, sowing the seeds of discord; and as the consequence of all this, she is suspected, shunned, dreaded, neglected, and has not a sincere friend on earth. The other is industrious, a *keeper at home*, peaceful, charitable, kind; and as the natural consequence of this, she is respected, esteemed, beloved, and finds a friend in every virtuous heart. Behold the fruits of idleness, in the one case, and avoid it; see the fruits of laudable industry, in the other, and pursue it. Obey the earnest command and exhortation of Paul, intended to prevent idleness with all its numerous and disastrous effects: *Now them that are such* [idlers, busy-bodies,] *we command and exhort, by our Lord Jesus Christ, that with quietness they work, and eat their own bread.*

Idleness is particularly dangerous to youth. At this interesting period the mind should be disciplined by regular attention to some useful occupation; the character should be formed, and habits acquired, which will promise usefulness and respectability in future. At this season the thoughts are naturally vagrant, the passions are warm and impetuous, and readily follow the wayward thoughts which excite them. The more the mind is left without the influence of wholesome restraint, the more it loves this kind of freedom, and the more impatient of control does it become. When the youth applies to his daily pursuit, not from inclination, nor from a sense of his own interest, nor from confirmed habit, but merely from a regard to the authority of his parents or instructors, the effects of idleness for one month, or even one week, will be very perceivable. The loss will be, not simply in proportion to the number of days or hours for which attention has been suspended, but also in proportion to the dissipation of thought, which has been the result of this intermission. At the end of this month or week the mind will not return to its regular pursuit with the same facility of application, with the same force of habit, which it possessed at the commencement. The boatman, ascending the stream, who intermits his exertions for ten minutes, will have lost, not simply the distance which he could have ascended in that time, but the distance also by which the current has carried him farther from the point of his destination: several minutes will be required to reach the point where his efforts ceased. The youthful mind is carried forward chiefly by authority operating on it from without, and not by motives which exist within itself. The moment authority ceases to operate, the mind is borne away by the current of its own thoughts and passions in a different, and most probably, in an opposite direction; time is, therefore, required to regain the point from which it has thus been carried away.

Now, if we are not greatly mistaken, this shows the reason why many a youth is ruined, who might have been a respectable and useful member of society, and a comfort to his friends—an injudicious exercise of this authority. It is absolutely a burlesque on human nature to suppose, as some, claiming the character of philosophers, have done, that a child is not to be subjected to any control, but be left to its own reason for a guide; as this strengthens, it is alleged, it will more and more clearly perceive and pursue the correct course. Long before reason can be supposed to have reached that maturity which would answer this purpose, thought is awakened, and passions are called into exercise. These passions are the current by which the mind is first moved. The child has yet no reason to guide this current, and the philosophy of the father will not permit his reason to interpose; the current is, therefore, suffered to take its own course. These passions are all to be indulged, for denial would be the exercise of authority, and every indulgence increases their strength. When reason, at length, casts its first feeble view on the world, through which it is to guide the child, the youth, and the man, it sees that world not as it really is, but as it appears through the perverting medium of the passions. Reason begins to unfold and to act under the full and established influence of the passions. If the reason of the father, with all his knowledge and experience of the world, did not attempt to control these passions, can the reason of the child be expected to turn their strong and impetuous current? The singularity of this philosophy is, that the child, whose passions are strong, whose reason is weak, whose knowledge of the world is extremely limited, should be expected to accomplish a task which the father, whose reason is fully matured, whose knowledge of the world, both from observation and experience, is extensive, has not attempted to do. The first conclusions of reason in the child will most probably be of this nature— My father who loves me, and who is much better qualified than I am to judge of the course I should pursue, has never denied, but always indulged me; I therefore conclude that this is the proper course. Reason comes into exercise—the pupil, or rather the subject of the passions. The reports which the understanding receives from the world without, of what is right and wrong, good and evil, honourable and dishonourable, proper and improper, are all made by the passions. These reports are the materials with which reason forms its first decisions; and it is easy to see that they will be in favour of the passions: indeed, according to the constitution of the human mind, they cannot be otherwise. A character formed on the principles of this philosophy, is one governed by the passions; reason has no other province, in fact, is permitted to do nothing else, than to devise ways and means for the indulgence of these sovereigns of the mind. Yet some profess to admire this system as a great improvement in education—as a method calculated to raise the human mind to the highest point of perfection, and thus promote, by rapid strides, the prosperity and happiness of society. We have known a few characters formed after this model; and certainly we could not envy the parents the satisfaction they derived from the experiment;

nor could the community very loudly boast of them as a valuable acquisition. A few weeks, during the late revolution in France, exhibit, on a large scale, the genuine tendency of this philosophy. May the loud trumpet of the angel summon this world to its last account, before another such exhibition is witnessed! You might as well take the reins of civil government from the enlightened and the wise, and place them in the hands of the ignorant, headstrong rabble, and call this a great improvement in political science. You might as well require a man to view every object through an instrument composed of glasses highly discoloured, and of different convexities, and call this a wonderful improvement in optics. You might as well deprive the ship of its compass and its rudder, leave it to drive before the wind and the tide, and call this a great improvement in navigation. Neither of these cases involves a greater absurdity than it does to withdraw entirely the judicious exercise of parental authority, and commit the government of a child to its own blind and impetuous passions.

Either in conformity with this preposterous theory, or from criminal and inexcusable negligence, parental authority often interposes at a period entirely too late to produce any good results. When the character has received its cast; when habits are formed; when the thoughts have taken their direction; when the passions are confirmed in unresisted dominion; the restraints of interposing authority will be spurned away; and the attitude of defiance, which the youth himself will, no doubt, call noble independence, will be assumed. It is now too late to mould the character into any other form than that which the passions will give it. The gentle rill may easily be led into another channel; but when swollen into an impetuous torrent, it defies such efforts, and rushes forward in its accustomed course. This youth is the disturber and the pest of schools and academies, and the patron of tumult and rebellion in colleges. Reaching the years of manhood, without mental discipline to render him useful, without virtuous principle to restrain him, he lives only to gratify his licentious passions. This indulgence is sought, regardless of the rights, the peace, or the happiness of others. His example spreads around him a contagion more dangerous than that of the most deadly disease. Female innocence and honour are never safe in his presence; they will be destroyed for his indulgence without hesitation and without compunction. The life of his most intimate friend will be sacrificed to gratify the pride of his haughty and resentful spirit. He moves through society like a volcano; the bursting forth of his passions will blast every vestige of virtue within its reach, and whelm in indiscriminate ruin every thing that stands in the way.

Sometimes this authority commences at a period sufficiently early; but it is too feeble to produce any good effect. The child soon learns to estimate the strength of that arm by which it is to be governed; and by a few trials, will ascertain the degree of importunity and perseverance which will obtain permission to take its own course. A system of judicious rules is laid down, but not enforced with sufficient firmness: the child soon learns the art of transgressing with impunity, and of obtaining the forbidden indulgence. The parent may think that he is discharging his duty; but the child is its own governor: there is the name and the appearance of authority, but not the reality. The only habit formed in the child, is the habit of seeking and contending for its own indulgence. The authority of others is irregular and capricious. One day it is exercised with decision; but the next, it is in a great measure, if not entirely, relaxed. The child, while under the influence of this authority, is anticipating the hour of relaxation, when it will enjoy the freedom of unrestrained indulgence. All that is gained one day is lost the next; no habit of regular application, or of submission is formed. One day authority urges the child forward in the correct course; the next, it is led by inclination and passion. These fluctuating efforts are not calculated to form a character for usefulness or respectability. There are others who exercise their authority only under the impulse of anger or resentment, which they either cannot, or do not take pains to conceal. Correction is sometimes administered with a severity altogether disproportioned to the fault; a slight offence is sometimes harshly reprimanded, while at another time, one of more dangerous tendency, under a less degree of feeling, is suffered to pass with impunity. The child soon learns to associate this authority, not with its own advantage, but with the gratification of the parent. It is not taught to consider its own passions as worthy of blame or correction; but the parent's irritation is blamed and regretted as the only obstacle in the way of its unbounded pleasure. Such a government, dictated, not by reason, nor by that *wisdom which cometh down from above*, but by the displeasure and resentment of the parent, will issue in no happy result; for *the wrath of man worketh not the righteousness of God*. To such authority the youthful mind will submit with the greatest impatience, and the hour of escape from its unwelcome restraints will be anticipated with eager delight, as the hour of freedom, independence, and happiness. That hour will come before this youth is prepared, by proper discipline of mind, by habits of application, industry and self-control, for a life of usefulness and respectability.

Many a youth, otherwise promising, is materially injured, and not a few are utterly ruined, by some radical defect in the training of their early years. Application to any regular business is, to them, irksome and intolerable. The gratification of their passions, the supreme law of their life, cannot be obtained without invading the rights, disturbing the peace, and destroying the happiness of others.

We cannot but notice the wisdom and goodness of those precepts of the Bible which relate to the education of children. They are adapted to what human nature has been found to be in all countries and in all ages. Instead of countenancing the opinion that the infant mind is a mere blank, without tendency to either good or evil, and susceptible of impressions alike from both, we are taught that from the very birth, the mind is depraved, or has a decisive tendency to that which is wrong; that its very first actings and emotions are evil. For several years the child is utterly incapable of governing itself; yet during these years, much of the arduous and difficult task of education may be accomplished, by forming habits of cheerful submission to the dictates of parental wisdom and prudence. The Bible recognizes the parent, under whose care the child is placed, as the person whose duty it is to perform this task. The great object which the parent should aim to accomplish, is the judicious control of the passions. In most cases, it is easier, and requires less effort, to prevent passion, than to manage and subdue it when excited. When they are excited, and this, after all the caution which can be used, will too often be the case, parental authority should interpose and prevent their indulgence. *Fathers, provoke not your children to anger.* The wisdom and goodness of this precept is forgotten or disregarded by those who, for their own amusement, unnecessarily tease and provoke children to fretfulness and anger. These persons may be amused with such needless irritation of the child; but they are doing it a serious injury, rendering the task of the parent more difficult, and are violating the precept of God. Passions once excited, will more easily be excited again; and the more frequently they are roused, the more violent and the more unmanageable do they become. Parents, provoke not your children, *lest they be discouraged.* If the authority of the parent is weak, capricious, exercised with evident displeasure, sometimes enforced and sometimes suspended, interposing with severity for mere trifles, the result of thoughtless indiscretion, and suffering more serious and designed offences to escape with impunity, the child will not know by what means to secure the approbation of the parent, will, of course, be discouraged, and give up the attempt as entirely hopeless. The whole duty of the parent is included in this precept—*Train up a child in the way in which it should go.*

With this view, authority should be exercised with constancy, with judgment, with decision, and yet with tenderness and affection. By persevering in this plan, through the aid of divine grace, the child will be trained and confirmed in the habit of willing and cheerful submission to authority; and this, we assuredly believe, however widely others may differ in opinion, is, at once, the most important and the most difficult part of education. When this habit is well established, the task of the instructor, either in literature or in the mechanical arts, will be easy and delightful. The man thus trained, accustomed to control his passions by the dictates of wisdom and prudence, will be prepared to render a cheerful obedience to the laws of the state; and, as far as human efforts can produce such an effect, will be prepared to bow to the high and holy authority of Heaven, the most reasonable, just, mild, and benign authority in the universe. This may be found a difficult task; but should not be given up in despair; *for it is the nurture and admonition of the Lord;* and the Lord will assist the honest efforts made in obedience to his will. The child thus trained up, *when he is old, he will not depart from it.*

By idleness, we mean the want of some regular and useful occupation, which, whether it gives exercise to the body or not, will certainly give exercise to the mind; will furnish habitual employment for the thoughts. The man whose thoughts are not thus employed, is idle; and idleness of this kind generally fosters the passions, and gives them a very pernicious and undue ascendency. There are some professions, indispensable to the good order and happiness of society, which give too little exercise to the body, and yet call for the utmost vigour of mental exertion. The man, engaged in these professions, may be most actively and usefully employed, and yet his body may even suffer for want of exercise. Such men deserve not the reproach of idleness. He is idle whose exertions are not calculated to increase the amount of human enjoyment. He who is inactive is the drone of society, feeding, without shame, on the labour of others: he who is active in wickedness infuses poison into the veins of society.

By industry we economize our time, gather up its fragments, and suffer nothing to be lost. The talent of turning every hour to some good account is a most desirable, because a most useful one. The amount of good resulting from the industry of a man, who improves these fragments of time, compared with one who, though not unemployed suffers them to be lost, will be very considerable, in the course of an ordinary life. Nor can any person, we conceive, plead an exemption from this obligation. If his own necessities do not require it, the suffering of others may be relieved by the fruit of this extra industry. From the sentence pronounced on man, immediately after the fall, it would appear that the comfortable subsistence of the human family, requires the labour and exertion, in some way or other, of every member of that family. If one is idle, some other one must, therefore, be taxed with more than his equal share of this labour. If one is found wasting the means of subsistence in the criminal indulgence of his passions and appetites, the want and suffering of another will be the consequence of this indulgence. Industry, economy, and charity should aim at equalising these toils and these sufferings.

SECTION II.

*Intemperance—Importance of Truth, Justice, Honesty—
Effects of Sinful Passions.*

INTEMPERANCE, often the consequence of idleness, is another pregnant source of human misery; all of which would be prevented by observing the wise and salutary precepts of the Bible. It is a proof of the divine goodness, that provision is made to satisfy the appetites of our animal nature; and a proof, not less obvious, of the same goodness is seen in prohibiting the indulgence of these appetites, beyond what nature requires. When sanctified by the word of God and prayer, and when received with thanksgiving, *every creature of God is good, and nothing to be refused.* But the moment these limits are disregarded, and our gratification is carried to excess, that moment it becomes pernicious to ourselves, and criminal in the sight of God. The law of Moses, given immediately from God himself, who is the author of our nature, and who knows what is inconsistent with our happiness, punishes with death a stubborn, rebellious, and intemperate son—Deut. xxi. 20: *If the parents shall say to the elders of the city, this our son is stubborn and rebellious, he is a glutton and a drunkard; all the men of the city shall stone him with stones that he die.* The will of God is good; and every departure from it will, sooner or later, be productive of misery, in proportion to this goodness. Intemperance is followed by a train of incalculable sufferings. It is open and deliberate rebellion against God; leads directly to poverty, wastes the health of the body, and destroys the life of thousands. Temperance, which is self-government, or moderation in the enjoyment of animal pleasures, is conducive to the health and vigour both of mind and body. *He that loveth pleasure shall be a poor man; he that loveth wine and oil shall not be rich; for the drunkard and the glutton shall come to poverty.* The observation of every person will convince him of the truth of these declarations. Hence the goodness of the following cautions, prohibitions, and warnings:— *Take heed to yourselves, lest at any time your hearts be overcharged with surfeiting and drunkenness and the cares of this world; when thou sittest to eat with a ruler, consider diligently what is before thee; and put a knife to thy throat, if thou be a man given to appetite: be not desirous of his dainties, for they are deceitful meats: let us walk honestly as in the day, not in rioting and drunkenness, not in chambering and wantonness: make no provision for the flesh to fulfil the lusts thereof: use this world as not abusing it.* The numerous and disastrous consequences of intemperance have proclaimed, and do loudly proclaim that goodness which exhorts us to be temperate in all things.

The intemperate use of ardent spirits, particularly, so frequently and so pointedly condemned in scripture, is an evil without a parallel in our beloved country. All the highway robbers, all the thieves, all the pilferers in the Union have not produced a tenth part of the misery which marks the progress of this insidious foe. All the flames which have threatened desolation to our cities, towns, and villages, have not destroyed a thirtieth, and probably not a fiftieth part, of what is wasted, and worse than wasted, by this demon of destruction. It generates some of the most painful diseases to which our system is liable; quenches the eye of genius in darkness, and degrades the most brilliant talents into mere drivelling childish imbecility: turns the wise man into a fool, and the peaceful and good-natured into furies of discord and contention. It destroys all sense of shame and moral obligation, and thus opens a wide door to every species of vice. It is the precursor of disputes, of quarreling, and feuds, which often terminate in bloodshed. *Who hath woe? who hath sorrow? who hath contentions? who hath babbling? who hath wounds without cause? who hath redness of eyes? They that tarry long at the wine; they that go to seek mixed wine.*

Intemperance can boast a greater number of

victims, and by far a greater amount of misery, than the sword of war. Could the calculation be accurately made, and was it to commence with the moment when the first American blood was shed on the plains of Lexington, embracing all whose life, during the revolutionary contest, was the price of our liberty; all who fell, by land and by sea, during the late war; all the trophies of the Indian tomahawk and scalping-knife; together with all the grief occasioned by these deaths in the bosom of surviving friends: and could a similar calculation be made, commencing from that moment down to the present, of all the deaths and all the sorrows occasioned by the intemperate use of ardent spirits, there is no doubt but the number of deaths would be greater, and the amount of grief more complicated and more poignant in the latter than in the former case. The records of every year, since that time, of every city, every town, every village, and every neighbourhood in our country would add to the catalogue of deaths and swell the amount of gloomy distress. During most of those years, the impliments of war have remained unemployed; but the angel of death has continued the work of destruction, by day and by night, without intermission.

The same effects may be expected, in time to come, from the same cause, unless it shall please a gracious God to arrest its progress. Let the miseries arising from this source, for twenty years to come, be grouped before the mind. You will, in that group, see the man, who, by correct deportment, by industry, and by temperance, rises to respectability and usefulness, sharing the merited esteem of numerous friends, seduced at length by this foe to the human race, tottering and falling, to rise no more; leaving a worthy family the victims of corroding sorrow, and the heirs of indigence and want. You will there see the young man, whose cultivated mind, whose promising talents, whose brilliant genius, have excited the joy of his parents and the hope of his friends, incautiously frequenting the haunts of intemperance, caught in the fatal snare, fast verging to disgrace, becoming a perfect nuisance in society, and rushing into a premature grave; exchanging the joy of his parents for anguish more intolerable than death, blasting the hope of his friends with all the bitterness of disappointment. How many wives will you there see, at the hour of midnight, to them a sleepless hour, suffering a torture increasing with every moment their husbands are absent, and yet dreading their return with apprehensions not less intolerable than this torture itself! How many children will you see, left orphans in a world of unfeeling neglect, doomed to a life of unpitied want, perhaps to beggary! The pencil of West has immortalized his name by adorning the canvass with the Saviour, giving strength to the feeble, limbs to the maimed, soundness to the lame, sight to the blind, and health to the sick. But of this group the figures requiring the strongest light, and claiming the most conspicuous place in the foreground; the insidious advances and desolating ravages of this monster; the convulsions of death, and the premature graves; the disappointed expectations and blasted hopes; the touching scenes of grief; the haggard forms of woe and despair, are too numerous and too complicated for the canvass to receive, and for the pencil of human skill to paint. Intemperance will hold the pencil; our country is the canvass where all these scenes will be exhibited: and Omniscience is the eye that will take them all in at one view. Let us beseech Almighty God to give success to his gospel—the only effectual remedy for all these nameless miseries.

The Bible not only requires the moral virtues of truth, justice, and honesty, but enforces them with all the authority of Heaven, and thus raises them to the rank of religious duties. From the frequency and earnestness with which these principles are inculcated, we may infer their beneficial tendency in promoting human happiness; observation and experience prove the correctness of this inference. We see and we feel the disappointment, the mischief, the embarrassment, the distress arising from misrepresentations intended to deceive, from wilful falsehood, from injustice, and fraud—all which evils would be prevented by a conscientious regard to the precepts of the Bible, which censures and condemns these vices—*Ye shall not lie one to another.* Putting away lying, speak every man truth with his neighbour. Lie not one to another, seeing ye have put off the old man. A righteous man hateth lying. Ye shall not steal, neither deal falsely. If thou sellest aught to thy neighbour, or if thou buyest aught of thy neighbour's hand, ye shall not oppress one another. The gospel teaches us to *live righteously; to do justice.* This is the will of God, that no man go beyond or defraud his brother in any matter, because that the Lord is the avenger of all such.

That departure from these evangelical principles which does the greatest mischief in society, is found in those who claim a respectable standing for truth and honesty; who would kindle with resentment at the insinuation that they were anything but men of strict veracity and justice. The notorious liar will deceive but few; for *a lying tongue is but for a moment.* The greatest injury is done to society, not, perhaps, by the thief and the robber, but by the numerous train of speculators, sharpers, swindlers, and those who carelessly or wilfully fail in fulfilling their promises, in complying with their contracts, in paying their debts. There are two classes of men whose honesty is not doubtful; the one embraces all those who never pay their just debts, until they are compelled by the civil law; the other, all those who *owe no man any thing,* who pay their debts punctually, and agreeably to their promise.

There is a third class, embracing, probably, a large majority, of whose honesty the best, perhaps, that can be said, is that it is doubtful. A obtains and appropriates to his own use the property of B, and promises that on a particular day he will make a satisfactory compensation to B for the use of his property. The promise is reduced to writing, is signed, and sealed, and witnessed. The specified day arrives which is to test the faithfulness and honesty of A; if the payment is made agreeable to promise, he is a man of sound integrity. Yet how often is it the case that the day arrives and passes away, and the payment is not made, the promise is not fulfilled. Where is the truth of this promise, and the justice of this delay? The promise was that B should receive his compensation on a particular day; but he does not receive it; of course the promise was not true. B consented that A should have his property without payment till a certain day, but no longer. Everyday, therefore, after the one specified, which A delays the payment, he holds this property not only without, but contrary to the consent of B. Can this be justice? If it be, what, then, is injustice? Our opinions on these subjects may be thought old-fashioned; we know, indeed, they are not fashionable, because they are not very common. But in our humble opinion, there is neither truth in this promise, nor justice in this transaction. Nor can we deem it a sufficient excuse for A to allege that he was ready, on the appointed day, to make the payment, if B had called on him for this purpose. It is, at least, implied in the promise of A, that he will go to B for this purpose. Still less satisfactory is the plea of forgetfulness. If he was to receive the payment, his memory, in all probability, would not be so treacherous. If truth and justice are matters of so much indifference with him, that he can so easily forget them, it is evident he is but little concerned to deserve the character which he claims. If A, when he made the promise, depended, for the means of fulfilling it, on his own industry and economy, and he, at the same time, is idle and wasteful, he is culpable, of course, in the same proportion; such idleness and prodigality cause the forfeiture of his fidelity and honesty. He indulges himself at the expense of another, contrary to his consent. After the promise is made, and before the day arrives, if any occurrence should take place, which A could neither prevent nor foresee, and which puts it out of his power to comply with this engagement, then he is clear of suspicion; provided, as soon as possible, he makes B fully acquainted with the fact: the failure is owing to the providence of God, not to his want of principle. If, however, no such event has occurred; if all the resources on which he depended have answered what might have reasonably been expected from them; or if he made the promise without any reasonable prospect, known at the time, of being able to comply with it; then, in addition to falsehood and injustice, no ingenuity nor even sophistry, can save him from the charge of wilful deception. Had these improbabilities and uncertainties been known, B would not, at least on the same terms, have given him possession of his property, nor placed the same confidence in his promise. This concealment, therefore, was fraudulent and criminal. It is not *walking honestly to them who are without*, nor who are within the church. It is not *providing things honest in the sight of all men*, still less *in the sight of the Lord our Judge*.

B makes a similar promise to C, and trusts in the fidelity and honesty of A for the means of complying with his engagement. C, placing confidence in B, makes a promise to D, and D again to E, and E to F, and so on. If A deceives B, the failure with all its consequences will roll on to C, and from C to D, and to E, and to F. F is urged for payment which he cannot make without a sacrifice. He is perplexed and embarrassed, and his property is sold for one third of its value. F commences a similar process with E, and E with D, &c., all of whom are involved in trouble and loss. Each of them have families who are involved in the same troubles; and whose reasonable expectations of future support and provision are blasted. Had A been a man of truth, and honesty, all this trouble and distress would have been prevented. Had the precepts of the gospel governed his heart and his life, he would have spoken the truth and acted honestly.

This case is the representative of ten thousand others which bear to it a greater or less degree of similarity, and produce greater or less degrees of those evils which always attend the violation of truth and justice. We know, indeed, that a thousand excuses will be offered to shield the character from the charge of falsehood and fraud. This proves that there is an indifference, truly alarming towards the authority of God, and to all that portion of human happiness which depends on the influence of truth and justice. The very excuse that is offered, does homage to the high importance and beneficial tendency of these sacred principles. He who offers it, wishes to enjoy the advantages and the pleasures which he supposes may be obtained by falsehood and dishonesty, while he shrinks from the reproach they deserve. The person who is the guilty cause of miseries extending beyond his knowledge, perhaps to generations yet unborn, lulls himself into indifference, and quiets his mind with the most frivolous excuse. *As a madman who casteth firebrands, arrows, and death; so is he that deceiveth his neighbour, and saith, am not I in sport?* As if society ought to suffer without complaint, for the pleasure of a base and fraudulent deceiver.

One day, or one week later than the time specified, in performing a promise, is considered a matter of too little consequence to deserve any blame. This, however, is as certainly a departure from truth as would be the delay of ten weeks or of ten years.

One drop contains all the properties of water as certainly as does the whole ocean; for the whole ocean is made up of single drops. One inch from a given line is as certainly a departure from that line as ten inches, or even twenty miles are. Add inch to inch, and at length you will make up the twenty miles, which consist of a definite number of inches. The greatest instance of falsehood, and which affects most deeply the interests of society, differs not in nature, but only in degree, from falsehood relating to small matters. If one day involves no blame, neither does two, nor four, nor eight, nor any definite number you please to mention. Add together as many cyphers as you please, and the amount will still be nothing. If one day involves no blame, neither does a year, nor even ten years, which are made up of a certain number of days. The injustice is more flagrant, the falsehood is more palpable and pernicious in proportion to the time for which the fulfilment of the promise is delayed; of course, each day, the first, as well as every other, has its due proportion of blame. Sound integrity of character is a unit; it cannot bear the slightest diminution, without injury.

The violation of matrimonial vows is attended with a train of evils which it is not easy to express, though thousands are doomed to writhe under them. The bare suspicion of infidelity fills the bosom with disquietude, and preys, like a vulture, on the heart; the proof of guilt destroys the happiness and embitters the future life of the injured party. The magnitude of the mischief arising from this species of unfaithfulness, is literally incalculable. The loss of affection, once solemnly pledged, the cold neglect, the bitter disappointment, the cruel insult, which is involved in every case of conjugal falsehood, make up the complicated injury, bequeathed to the miserable sufferer. The breach of this promise has in it all that is calculated to give aggravation to guilt in the sight of God, and all that is calculated to give poignancy to grief in the human heart. The promise of fidelity is generally, and ought universally to be made as the result of affections, excited and cherished by the view of qualities, at once amiable and desirable in their object; it is generally accompanied with those religious ceremonies which bring the parties to recognize their invisible Judge as the witness of their mutual sincerity. The deliberate and wanton violation of such a promise is marked with a dereliction of principle, and with a turpitude of character which cannot easily be surpassed; and is productive of that complicated anguish which can find no refuge, and admits of no relief in this world. Even the kind hand of religion cannot pluck this thorn from the heart, and heal the wound which it inflicts. The grave is the only refuge to which the victims of this base infidelity can look for complete deliverance. Multitudes who are the authors of this exquisite suffering, who deserve the deepest brand of infamy, yet dare to show their shameless faces in decent society, and look for that respect which is due only to the virtuous and the good: and it is a melancholy proof of the want of correct principle, and of the low state of moral and religious feeling, that they do not meet, wherever they appear, those indignant frowns which would be too intolerable for them to bear.

No man can read the Bible without perceiving with what just severity this species of falsehood and injustice is censured and condemned. Criminals of this description generally disregard the discipline of the church; and for various reasons too often escape the penalties of the civil law: thus they pass with triumphant impunity. They can, however, escape but for a short time: such transgressors GOD WILL JUDGE: He alone can inflict a punishment proportioned to their guilt, and to the sufferings they occasion to others. If the frowns of society do not repulse them, the frowns of Jehovah will pursue them with everlasting disgrace.

Universal experience and observation will justify us in affirming that much, very much of the miseries of this life may be traced back to the sinful and wicked passions of men as their cause. By observing that darkness uniformly retires before the rising sun, and returns again when he is withdrawn, we conclude that the sun is the cause of light, and of day, and that darkness is the consequence of his absence. In like manner, by observing that suffering, in a greater or less degree, is the concomitant of these guilty passions, we infer that the one is the cause of the other.

The bosom in which these passions exist is not and cannot be happy. The proud man is not happy. He spurns with contempt the adulation of the vulgar, as unworthy of his notice; his pride is nourished by the approbation of those alone, whose weight of character has raised them to the more elevated grades in society. Hence those who can minister to his gratification are comparatively but few; and of this few, many of them will be his competitors for public applause. Two men governed by the spirit of pride, are said to be the most disagreeable companions to each other. They advance their mutual claims to meet with mutual denial and disappointment. Each one expects to receive what the other is not disposed to give. Pride is ever ready to receive, but never to bestow approbation; except, perhaps, with the view of receiving the same in return, with more than legal interest. This, however, is more the artifice of that paltry kind of pride, called vanity, than of that lofty, though diabolical feeling of which we are speaking. Vanity, which feeds on the flattery of all without discrimination, and soon recovers from the pain of disappointment, is the feature of a weak mind: pride is the vice of a great mind, and can relish nothing but that applause which is unconstrained and sincere. The slightest suspicion that the incense offered on its shrine is nothing but mere formality, not seasoned with sincerity, produces the bitterest disappointment and chagrin. If he sees others receiving those respectful acknowledgments which he covets, this excites in his bosom jealousy, envy, hatred, malice, and resentment; passions which, like a host of furies, prey upon his peace. Proud men are not disposed to gratify him, because they consider him their rival and opponent; men of real worth are not disposed to gratify him, because they consider it wrong to furnish indulgence for any vicious passion. Hence, his arrogant claims meeting with repulses from every quarter, his haughty spirit becomes, in his own breast, a source of vexation and disquietude. God and man agree in this one thing; that is, in *resisting the proud*. If there is on earth a human being whom you could wish to see devoid of peace, and unhappy, infuse into him the spirit of pride, and your object will be accomplished.

The ambitious man is not happy: his insatiable spirit, like the daughters of the horse-leech, is continually crying, *give, give;* and like the grave, never saith, *it is enough*. He enters the public arena with numerous competitors, who labour to elevate themselves by thrusting him down. They scrutinize his character, suspect his motives, call in question his talent, thwart all his purposes, and view him as a public and licensed mark for the shafts of slander and reproach. Viewing them with the troubled eye of jealousy and envy, he contends with the same weapons, and employs the same methods for his own advancement, and derives the same enjoyment from their discomfiture. Through these tumultuous conflicts, along this perilous path, he urges his way towards the object of desire. Every ascent which he gains increases his desire, and redoubles his efforts to rise still higher. At length his eye fixes on the very summit of fame, and on the very highest post of honour, as the only limit of his boundless ambition. Nothing below this summit will quiet his restless spirit; and if this should, at length, be attained, a thousand bitter recollections of the past ascend with him as the inmates of his bosom; a thousand suspicions and jealousies respecting the motives and designs of others invade him; the envy of disappointed rivals, in a thousand forms and degrees haunt him, like spectres from the dead, and disturb his peace. The happiness which he fondly anticipated has fled from the station which he fills, and has left him heir to a nameless train of corroding anxieties. That ambition which increased as he advanced, is now greater than at any former stage; and yet having no higher object on which it can fix, it therefore becomes the tormentor of the bosom in which it exists. Such a mind can no more be at peace than can the ocean under the influence of the rushing tempest.

If ambition dwells in the bosom of a chief, or a sovereign, his neighbours of the same grade become the objects of his suspicion and his jealousy. If they are his superiors, then his wealth, his power, his royalty, avail him nothing, till he can equal them; this accomplished, his spirit cannot rest till he is their acknowledged superior. When the world is obsequious at his feet, he weeps that there are not more worlds in the same prostrate condition.

There is another passion which torments the bosom in which it is cherished; that is, avarice. This is not only sinful in the sight of God, but it is ridiculous in the sight of men. The man who is under the domination of this vice is necessarily unhappy. He feels a desire for the increase of his wealth which cannot be satisfied; and all ungratified desire, of this kind particularly, is suffering. *He that loveth silver, shall not be satisfied with silver; neither he that loveth abundance, with increase.* He loves wealth for its own sake, not as the means of innocent enjoyment, and still less of doing good. He prohibits himself from the enjoyment of it with a vigilance scarcely less constant and severe, than that with which he guards it from others. Supposing that the idol of his heart is as precious to others as it is to himself, he is the victim of perpetual fear and dread, lest it should be wrested from him by the hand of violence. Though he dare not enjoy it, yet its safety is, to him, a source of the most anxious solicitude. *The abundance of the rich will not suffer them to sleep.* Nor does he consider, *for whom do I labour, and bereave my soul of good?* His mean and sordid soul would be worthy of contempt, if his wretchedness and guilt did not advance much stronger claims to commiseration.

The man who is under the influence of envy cannot be happy. The good, the advantage, the enjoyment of others, especially of rivals and superiors, is the object of this feeling. The man voluntarily becomes his own tormentor because others are happy. Their deprivation, their misery, is the only relief his sufferings will admit of. It is said that Omnipotence can accomplish whatever is possible: is it possible, then, for God, who is infinite in goodness, and who delights in happiness, to create a rational creature who can be happy while envy is a feature of his character? If he could, the fact is beyond our comprehension. He, therefore, who cherishes this passion must feel the suffering which it inflicts; there is no escaping from it. *Envy slayeth the silly one: envy is the rottenness of the bones.*

The sufferings which result from anger, are obvious to all men. The world could not persuade you that the man under its influence is otherwise than unhappy. The flashing of his eye, his incoherent and hurried speech, his agitated frame, will force on your mind the conviction that, both in mind and body, he is suffering. Death is said to have been the consequence, in some instances, of violent paroxysms of this passion; and in many others, it is said to shorten life by generating painful and dangerous diseases. "Anger is particularly injurious to infants, who, from the sensibility of their frames, are extremely susceptible of this passion, and are sometimes so severely afflicted as to die suddenly in convulsions, or to retain ever after an imbecility of mind and body arising from its powerful impression. We ought as rational agents to beware of encouraging such destructive emotions; for it is certain that men and women possessing an irascible temper generally die of pulmonary consumptions; and young persons, especially females, should be informed, that independently of its moral turpitude, it deforms the face, steals the rose from the cheek of beauty, and not only tends to extinguish the most tender affections, but sometimes even produces aversion. It is only, therefore, *in the bosom of fools* that *anger resteth;* of those who are regardless of their own peace of mind, of their own health and the preservation of their own lives. If the various modifications of this passion, malice, resentment, revenge, &c., be less violent, they are for that very reason more permanent. These are the forms into which anger frequently subsides; and they keep the mind in a state of habitual irritation and uneasiness until they are satiated by the infliction of punishment on their object. The effect of these passions on the peace and tranquillity of the mind is greater, because it is uniform. The malevolent spirit is continually watching and secretly praying for the calamity of its object; and if this calamity is escaped, painful disappointment is the consequence. Revenge is not satisfied with merely watching for calamity; it devises ways and means for producing misfortune. Like a beast of prey, its enjoyment and its life consist in the pain and death of others; and for the sake of this enjoyment, it will inflict this pain and this death.

There is a host of minor feelings which keep the mind in a state of perpetual disquietude, like the troubled sea which cannot rest. The mind is sometimes torn and vexed with what may be called the dregs of other sinful and tormenting passions. Discontentedness renders the person dissatisfied with everything in his present condition; peevishness renders him fretful and disobliged with the kindest efforts to please; caprice is teased and provoked by the very things which, a few minutes before, had been wished for; ill-nature ferments and turns the spirits to acid and to gall. These feelings, like ulcers, destroy the peace of the mind, and keep it in a state of habitual and painful irritation; and, to the eye of nice and correct moral perception, they deform the character, and strip it of all its loveliness, as certainly as ulcers do the features of the countenance.

Of these passions, it may be observed, that there is an affinity between them; they very naturally and almost necessarily generate each other. Pride and ambition almost always produce envy and jealousy. The cause of disappointed expectations will be construed into insults and injuries; and thus anger, malice, resentment, and revenge will be excited. Under the frequent excitement and corrosion of these passions, the mind is disposed to discontent, peevishness, and caprice; and thus ill-nature and harshness of temper become permanent features of character.

The man who cherishes these passions is sure to suffer the consequence of his own folly. There is in his own bosom an operative cause of vexation and torment, from which he cannot escape. He may change his circumstances in life; he may change his pursuit; he may change his friends; but, until his heart is changed, by the grace of God, he must and will be an unhappy man.

While these passions are tormenting the heart in which they exist, they are the cause of a nameless train of miseries to mankind. War is one of the most dreadful scourges with which the indignation of insulted Heaven has ever visited our guilty globe. Probably nine-tenths of the wars which have been waged have been owing to the pride, ambition, revenge, or lawless cupidity of those called chiefs, rulers, or sovereigns of the people whom they were permitted to afflict. Calculate the consequences of one single conflict. Take your station in that field, soon to be stained with the blood of thousands. See the two armies advancing to meet each other; think of the art and ingenuity with which their implements have been fitted for the work of slaughter and death; think of the talents and military prowess with which all the arrangements have been made. View the mingled emotions of apprehensive dread and determined courage with which they advance: see the countenance at one moment brightening with the hope of victory; the next overcast with a momentary pensiveness, from a glance of thought on the friends left at home. The signal is given, and the work of destruction begins. Blood, and groans, and death strike your ear and meet your view on every side. The conflict over, suppose yourself the messenger of these tidings of sorrow to the friends of those whose agonies and death you have witnessed. Go to the cottage and tell the mother of a helpless family that she is a widow, and her children are fatherless; that you saw the husband whom she loved in the agonies of death, and heard him, with his last breath, commend her and her orphan children to the kind protection of Heaven. Gauge the misery of this cottage, and then multiply it by all the thousands who are made widows and left fatherless on the same day. Go to the parents, whose son, the joy of their heart, and the hopes of their declining years, is lifeless on the field; tell them that you saw him fall by the hands of a man whom he never had injured, and towards whom he cherished not one unfriendly feeling; that he died trodden under foot by triumphant enemies, without one kind office or one cheering word of friendship

THE INFLUENCE OF THE BIBLE. 125

to soothe his last moments. Witness the depth of sorrow into which these parents are plunged, and multiply this by all the parents who receive the same tidings from this field of blood. Ask yourself, what is the cause of all these groans, of these agonies of death, of this incalculable amount of grief in the heart of surviving friends? It is to gratify the ambition, or some other guilty passion, of one single man: this passion is the mainspring which moves this machinery of anguish. Had this man possessed the mild, the humble, the peaceful spirit of the gospel, all this misery would have been prevented.

Would you see a particular case in which these remarks are exemplified? From the smouldering ruins of Moscow follow the retreat, or rather flight, of the French army; witness all the complicated sufferings which distinguish that flight, and you will see them exemplified. To the restless spirit, to the insatiable ambition of one man, is all that suffering to be ascribed. Had this man been contented with the empire of France, of which he was the acknowledged sovereign, he might have left it as an inheritance to his posterity. But Alexander reigned in the north without doing vassalage to him. This preyed upon his peace, and rendered his life unhappy. Ambition called out his numerous army, guided its march to Moscow, and thus gave rise to all the miseries which followed, and which, perhaps, have never been exceeded, except when the judgment of God fell on that devoted city, Jerusalem.

11 *

SECTION III.

Discontentedness, Peevishness—Pious Affections secure Peace of Mind.

The effects of anger, in disturbing the peace of society are well known. During the violence of this passion, the operations of reason are suspended, or her voice is not heard, and her dictates are disregarded. The proverb is not without truth, *ira brevis furor;* under the paroxysm of rage, man becomes a madman, is deprived of his understanding, and is impelled by blind and furious passions. Those things are often done which no future regret can ever repair. Death is frequently the consequence of this dangerous excitement; and death always carries anguish to the heart of surviving friends. The guilty homicide, if murderer is thought too harsh a term, may, in moments of cool reflection, weep bitterly over the result of his own passion; but this sorrow, however deep and sincere, will not restore the dead to life, nor heal the bleeding heart of sorrowing relations, though it may, in some measure, disarm them of their resentment. During the fit of anger, the restraint of the tongue is lost; and words, in a torrent, the most bitter and the most provoking, are uttered. These often produce deadly strife and contention, or fix in the heart deep-rooted animosities and hatred; feelings which the apology, suggested and offered in calmer moments, cannot efface; but which sometimes descend as an inheritance from father to son. If malice and revenge are less violent, they are not less dangerous to the peace of society. If they do not suspend the operations of reason, they employ that reason in devising means for the execution of their diabolical purposes. The paroxysms of anger are soon over; but these remain principles of action for days and for years. Anger gives indications of the threatening storm, and thus furnishes at least a moment for escape or defence; but these coolly deliberate on the means of punishment or death, and mature their plan, a part of which is, to conceal their design till it is ripe for execution, and thus leave no time for escape or defence. Malice and revenge are prominent features, active and permanent principles in the character of Satan; this renders him the more dangerous to us. The man who lives under the influence of these passions, not only proves, by a strong resemblance, his relationship to this fallen spirit, but, according to his power, is equally dangerous to the peace and happiness of mankind.

A vast amount of human happiness is destroyed by discontentedness, by peevishness, by sourness and harshness of temper. The explosions of anger, and the deep and secret designs of malice and revenge, are dreadful; but these make up what they want in violence by the frequency with which they recur. There are some who are habitual *murmurers, complainers*, who can be pleased with nothing, who are dissatisfied with every thing. A failure to gratify their whims and their desires, which they have not expressed, and which there was no possibility of knowing, is construed into designed neglect, insult, or cruelty. Your mildness, your gentleness, and kindness, only irritate their discontented spirits; perhaps, by forcing on their observation, from the contrast, the unwelcome picture of their own hearts. A mere trifle will furnish employment for their querulous tongues, determined never to be idle, till something else occurs to take its place. Never satisfied themselves, they disturb the peace of all around them. One kind look, one mild and gentle expression from them would be a phenomenon—something out of the ordinary course of things. Those who are confined within the range of their ill-natured and peevish loquacity, have great need of meekness, forbearance, and patience; for the grievances which they are doomed to suffer are of no small magnitude; grievances for which wealth and splendour can bring no alleviation. One such spirit is more than sufficient to keep a whole family in constant agitation and disquietude. *Better is a dinner of herbs where love is, than a stalled ox and* hatred therewith. *A continual dropping in a very rainy day, and a contentious woman, are alike. It is better to dwell in a corner of the house top, than with a brawling woman in a wide house. It is better to dwell in the wilderness, than with a contentious and angry woman. The contentions of a wife are a continual dropping.* Whether the proverbs of Solomon are the result of experience, or of observation, or of both, we cannot tell, nor is it material; for the testimony of all ages confirms their truth. In every age, the plain simple meal, with kindness and love, has been preferred to the sumptuous feast with ill-nature, animosities, strife, and hatred. In every age, the repose of the solitary wilderness has been preferable to the wide house, filled and disturbed in every part with the clamorous voice of a peevish, discontented, and brawling woman. In every age, the quietness of an obscure corner in the house-top has been a desirable refuge from the keen and ceaseless contentions of a scolding wife. Females have the right, and are perfectly justifiable in exercising this right, of reversing these proverbs, and applying them to the male sex. Many a wife is suffering, in secret, under the ill-nature, the sulky harshness of an unfeeling and tyrannical husband; suffering, too, when prudence restrains her from pouring her tale of woe into the bosom of the most confidential and intimate friend, and thus seeking that relief which sympathy affords. Many a husband seeks to gratify his contentious and cowardly spirit by the keenness of his wit, by the biting and reproachful sarcasm, by the sly and invidious hint, or by the boisterous torrent of coarse and vulgar abuse, directed against the wife of his bosom, whose peace and happiness he is bound to promote, and whom gentleness and meekness restrain from attempting to retaliate the injuries she suffers. If two such rugged and fiery spirits should be connected in matrimony, the discord, and strife, and misery of the family, whose mornings are ushered in with the signal for contention, and whose evenings find that contention unfinished, would give a fearful resemblance to that region from which all goodness, and gentleness, and meekness, and forbearance are banished; where every feature of sin has reached a dreadful maturity; where they are *hateful, and hating one another;* where they are employed in making each other as miserable as possible; where the wailings of disappointment, the groans of anguish and despair, is the music which leads on the march of eternal existence.

Who can look on the world, agitated and afflicted as it is with these restless and guilty passions, without breathing to Heaven an ardent desire for some remedy that will restore peace to the mind, relieve mankind from the evils which they suffer from this source? The Bible is that remedy. No sooner does its divine light shine into the understanding— no sooner does its sacred truth impress the heart, than a change commences, which, in its progress, tends to peace and happiness. The proud man becomes humble; the ambitious man becomes moderate in his expectations and desires; envy and jealousy wither and die with the root which nourishes them; the avaricious man gives up his idol, and raises his affections to God; anger is displaced by meekness; malice, resentment, and revenge, by forbearance, the forgiveness of injuries, brotherly kindness and charity; the discontented, ill-natured, peevish, murmuring, querulous spirit becomes contented, mild, gentle, good-natured, and benevolent. Destroy these evil passions and tempers, and you prevent all the misery and disquietude which they produce; excite, in their stead, these friendly and devout affections, and those who cherish them will enjoy peace within, become useful members of society, and contribute, in no small degree, to the happiness of all with whom they are connected.

The truth of God has, in itself, a powerful tendency to produce these effects; and the Spirit of God renders it effectual in the commencement and progress of this change. Pride is the offspring of ignorance: remove this ignorance, and you remove with it the pride to which it gives rise. The knowledge and belief of the truth is the only remedy for ignorance. The proudest man on earth would soon be humble, if he could see the sinfulness and vileness of his own heart, as it is represented in the word of God. Though he might excel thousands of others in talents, in learning, and in wealth, yet under the clear light of truth, he would see that these things shrink into nothing, as it regards his relation to God, and are no foundation for that exalted idea of his own importance, which he formerly entertained. In the glass of the gospel he will see himself possessed of other features of character than those which he had been accustomed to contemplate, with so much self-gratulation; features which not only expose him to deserved punishment, but also to merited shame and disgrace. Viewing his numerous and criminal deficiencies when tried by the laws of God, the only correct and infallible standard, he begins *to think soberly of himself, and not more highly than he ought to think.* Ambition is fed by a false estimate respecting the distinctions of this world, of its power, its honour, and its fame. So very erroneous are his views, that his chief happiness consists in obtaining these distinctions. Correct this error, and his ambitious spirit assumes another aspect. Truth is not only the remedy for ignorance, but also the antidote of error. Let him learn from the pages of the Bible the real value of worldly distinctions; let him learn from the same source the infinite importance of that *honour which cometh from God,* of the approbation of his Almighty Judge, and the objects alone on which that approbation can fix, and his desire for worldly distinctions will be graduated by the scale of truth; he will *labour that whether present or absent,* whether in this, or in the world of spirits, *he may be accepted of Him whose favour is life.* Whatever be the origin and component parts of avarice, it is branded in Scripture with the guilt and turpitude of idolatry; it is robbing God of those affections which are his due, and placing them on objects which do not deserve them. Under the influence of truth, the avaricious man will feel and acknowledge that he is not the independent proprietor, but the responsible steward of his possessions. Penetrated with this conviction, he will feel his accountability for the use he makes of this wealth; and will value it chiefly as the means of doing good, of relieving the wants of the suffering, and of promoting the kingdom of Christ. He will see that *the love of money is the root of all evil;* and will *set his affecions on things above, not on things on the earth.* Anger is most effectually prevented by the considerations presented to the mind in the gospel. It is less deliberative, less manageable than either of the preceding passions. Sometimes, indeed, it rushes on the mind like an impetuous torrent, and hurries it into purposes of revenge, without time for a moment's reflection. Generally, however, it is progressive, though this progress is very rapid. It is excited by a sense of injury either received or apprehended. The first excitement spreads its own colouring over the provocation, and greatly magnifies the cause of offence. During the paroxysm, all thoughts but those suggested by the real or supposed injury are driven from the mind; and it is deaf alike to the dictates of its own reason, and to the remonstrances of friendship. If you would guard the mind from the influence of this painful and dangerous excitement, you must carefully guard against the very first irritating impression. Strongly associate with the sense of injury, those considerations which have a powerful tendency to counteract and prevent the very first feelings of anger and resentment, and to preserve the mind tranquil and composed. In moments of calm reflection, prepare the mind, by storing it with these considerations, for the moment of provocation, as the moment of danger, when this aid will be necessary to preserve it in safety; and when, without care and this aid, it may be hurried into the most violent excesses. Now it is obvious to remark, that this is the very method observed, and these the very means employed in delivering the mind from the influence of anger and all its modifications, malice, resentment, and revenge. The deep impressions which the gospel makes on the heart, the materials of thought with which it supplies the mind, have a powerful tendency to check the first risings of anger, and thus to preserve that tranquillity which admits of useful reflection. The man who sees his own guilt in a true light; who feels himself arraigned before the bar of his Almighty Judge, and charged with numberless offences of the most provoking and aggravating nature; who feels in his own conscience the justice of that sentence which condemns him;

who, with earnest and humble importunity, prays to God that he would pardon his sins, and not punish him as he deserves; this man will not, with these impressions deeply fixed on his heart, with these recollections in his mind, turn round and seize a fellow-creature by the throat, demanding satisfaction for some trifling offence: he will leave the presence of his God with a spirit of meekness, and some degree of that forgiveness of injuries, on which he himself depends for the pardon of his guilt. He will thus be prepared to meet the various provocations of life with a calmness of reflection, with a shield of meekness, with a spirit of forbearance and forgiveness, which will disarm these provocations of their tendency to disturb his peace. He will see, from a moment's reflection, that some of these injuries are imaginary, and not real; others were not intended; others, though real, are but slight, and cannot affect his happiness by any means as much as his own irritation would certainly do; others which were intended, and which materially affect his happiness, as he hopes to be forgiven of God, he will *from the heart forgive, and commit himself to him who judgeth righteously.* That discontentedness, murmuring, peevishness, &c., which destroy so much of the peace and comfort of mankind, are weakened and finally swept away by the softening and improving influence of the gospel. The man who is discontented with his present condition, vents his ill nature on the friends who kindly try to please him, murmurs and frets under the slightest inconvenience to which he is subjected, will be cured of this unhappy spirit by an impressive view of his guilt and unworthiness, by perceiving how little he deserves from the hand of God or man; by the conviction that instead of the favours with which he is surrounded, and the kindness bestowed on him, he deserves the reproach and neglect of men, and the heavy displeasure of God. When the gospel is correctly understood and cordially received, it improves the heart, and elevates the mind above the littleness of these repinings and complaints.

The gospel prohibits, in the strongest terms, the exercise of these criminal passions; and enforces, with earnestness, the cultivation of pious, social, and devout affection. From a great number of passages to this effect, the following are offered:—"Pride and arrogance do I hate. Woe to the crown of pride. Love not the world, neither the things that are in the world. If any man love the world, the love of the Father is not in him; for all that is in the world, the lust of the flesh, the lust of the eye, and the pride of life, is not of the Father. Wherefore laying aside all malice, and all envies. Let us not be desirous of vain glory, provoking one another, envying one another. Let all bitterness and wrath, and anger, and clamour, and evil speaking be put away from you, with all malice. And be ye kind one to another, tender-hearted, forgiving one another, even as God for Christ's sake hath forgiven you. Be kindly affectioned one to another, with brotherly love. But now ye also put off all these: anger, wrath, malice, blasphemy, filthy communication out of your mouth. Put on, therefore, as the elect of God, holy and beloved, bowels of mercies, kindness, humbleness of mind, meekness, long-suffering; forbearing one another, and forgiving one another, if any man have a quarrel against any; even as Christ forgave you, so also do ye. And above all these things put on charity, which is the bond of perfectness. Dearly beloved, avenge not yourselves; but rather give place unto wrath. See that none render evil for evil unto any man. Be not overcome of evil, but overcome evil with good. Charity suffereth long and is kind; charity envieth not; charity vaunteth not itself, is not puffed up, is not easily provoked; beareth all things, believeth all things, hopeth all things, endureth all things." These, and such as these, are the precepts and doctrines, which, being received and obeyed by faith, strike their impression on the heart and form the moral character.

The structure of the human mind is a grand display of the wisdom of God; the gospel is also the wisdom of God; the one is, therefore, adapted to the other. It has already been stated that our passions and affections can be controlled only by our perceptions, thoughts, and conclusions. No man can awaken in his bosom the passion of anger, as he can move his hand, by a simple act of volition. He cannot feel resentment towards an object, which, in his apprehension, is perfectly harmless. Some degree of injury, either received or expected, is necessary to excite this feeling. Fear cannot be roused without apprehension of danger. The affection of love can never be called into exercise but by the view of something amiable, the contemplation of which will give pleasure, and the possession of which will give happiness. To this constitutional trait of the human mind, the gospel is wisely adapted. While it prohibits the exercise of these sinful passions, it pours a flood of light on the object which excite them; it shows these objects in their comparative littleness, and their insufficiency to afford the happiness expected from them; and thus, by divesting them of those properties which they were supposed to possess, the passions are weakened which they had excited. Diminish the cause, and you diminish the effect produced by that cause. While it requires us to cherish every devout and social affection, it presents to our view objects most worthy of these affections. If it requires us to love God supremely, it exhibits the infinite goodness of God as the object of this love. If it requires us to be thankful, it exhibits the *unspeakable gift*, it confers the unmerited favour, as the cause of this thankfulness. If it requires us to hope, it sets before us the atonement of a divine Saviour's death as the ground of this hope.

God be thanked, says Paul to the Romans, *that ye have obeyed from the heart that form of doctrine which was delivered you.* Some commentators understand him as representing the doctrines of the gospel as a mould, into which the mind is cast, and from which it receives its impressions; as melted metal, poured into a mould, receives all the impressions of that mould. The more closely the mind comes in contact with the gospel, the more deep and lasting will be its impressions. The more accurate and extensive our knowledge of the gospel becomes, and the more cordially we receive and obey it, the less will we be conformed to this world, and the more will we be transformed by the renewing of our mind; the more will this world be crucified to us, and we to the world; the more will we die unto sin, and live unto God; the more will we be renewed and improved in the spirit of our mind. If the gospel does not instantaneously, yet it does gradually and effectually, detach our affections from this world, and raise them to God, to the Saviour, and to things spiritual and divine. The farther the Christian advances under the guidance and power of the gospel, the more peace and happiness does he enjoy in his own heart; the more kind and affectionate does he become to his friends, and those who are immediately connected with him; the more useful does he become to the Church and to the world.

The Christian has peace in his own bosom. Compare the man who is *proud in spirit,* with the man who has *put on humbleness of mind*, and you cannot but see the difference. Pride requires for its nourishment the incense of adulation continually rising from its altar; with this nourishment it increases, and requires still more of this incense for its indulgence. Denied of this, it corrodes the bosom with suspicion, dissatisfaction, and jealousy; and finally turns to pure misanthropy. Its aspect is repulsive to all men; all find a secret delight in witnessing its mortification, chagrin, and disappointment. Humility, on the other hand, evangelical humility, is modest and conciliating. Advancing no claims for the notice and applause of this world, it is perfectly safe from the disquietude of disappointment and chagrin. Wherever it appears it proclaims peace within, and good will to men. Seeking and valuing chiefly the approbation of God, this can be enjoyed in retirement, remote from the strife and tumult of the world. With this approbation it increases: and the more it increases the more independent does it become of the admiration of this world. If there is peace on earth, it will be found in retirement, in the bosom that is *meek and lowly*.

Where shall we find a suitable contrast between the spirit of restless ambition, and that *moderation*, respecting the distinctions of this world, which characterizes every true Christian? Take Cæsar, at the moment when he had formed the resolution to pass the Rubicon:—Rather take an example of more recent date, over which antiquity has thrown less obscurity; take the late emperor of France, at the moment when the design of invading Russia is formed. His calculations are made; his diagrams are finished; his generals are named; his places of depot are appointed; the route of his army is prescribed; the first order is issued, and the first step is taken in execution of this design. At this moment, so eventful in his life, with what conflicting passions must not his mind have been agitatted and torn? At one moment he anticipates the glory of dictating terms of peace to Alexander, in the metropolis of his own empire; and then, as the consequence of this victory, sees, what he had not yet seen, England trembling at his triumphant progress; and, perhaps, casting his eye across the Atlantic, and adorning his brow with a few laurels from this country. But although a tide of almost uninterrupted success had attended his movements, yet no man knew better than he did the perils and hazards of war; he could not drive from his mind the possibility of a reverse; nor could he well avoid anticipating some of the consequences of this reverse; the glory already attained might be clouded; the throne on which he is seated might be shaken; the station which he now fills might be lost. Thus, although not one ray of prophetic light shone on the prospect before him, though he could not foresee that train of events which are now historical facts, yet he could not prevent these tremendous uncertainties, these painful per-adventures, from commingling with his more pleasing anticipations, and disturbing his peace. The blood which is to flow, the groans to be uttered, the pangs and tortures of death to be felt, the grief and anguish of surviving friends, gave him no uneasy sensation: for ambition is deaf and blind to these things. With this man contrast our beloved Washington, at the moment when he enters the hall of Congress, with the view of laying on their table the commission previously received from them. The toils and labours, the perils of war are past. His military prowess had been admired, even by his enemies; but this is the moment when his character appears in all its dignity, surrounded with a glory which Alexander, which Cæsar, which Bonaparte never attained. The independence of his country is acknowledged. There appears in his view a rising and expanding empire, the patroness of liberty, and the asylum for the distressed and the persecuted of all nations. Every feature of his countenance tells the noble and generous feelings of his heart. The recollection of past scenes, of the companions who fell by his side, of the sufferings he witnessed, awakens a sympathy which imparts a softness and tenderness to these manly feelings, and renders them still more interesting. Those hopes which animated and supported him through the hazards of the Revolution, are now realized; his peace of mind is undisturbed; his joy is pure and sublime. Bonaparte was a man of boundless ambition: Washington was a man of genuine, of tried patriotism; and, what is infinitely more, there is reason to hope he was a man of sincere piety. The design of this contrast is not invidious, but to enforce the divine precept; *Let your moderation be known to all men.* He who cherishes a spirit of ambition is sharpening a thorn to pierce his own heart.

The Christian, whose heart is thoroughly reformed, "neither envies nor grieves at the good of his neighbour;" the excellence and the happiness of others no longer subject him to the painful feelings of malignity and hatred towards them. Their happiness increases his own; he *rejoices with those who do rejoice.* His benevolence, his Christian charity, lead him to desire and pray for the happiness of all men; when his prayer is answered, he is thankful, not envious.

How calm and peaceful is the mind, guarded from the painful agitations of anger, wrath, malice, resentment, and revenge, by that meekness, forbearance, and forgiveness, which are features of every Christian character! The moment of provocation is the moment when those affections are required and called into exercise, and when they appear in their most amiable and attractive light. The greater the provocation, the more it would justify, in the world's estimation, the feelings of resentment, the more glorious is the triumph of the Christian in maintaining a sweet serenity and peace of mind. The man of wrathful spirit takes the work of vengeance into his own hands, and, driven by blind and furious passion, inflicts the punishment which resentment suggests. When this excitement has subsided, when he reviews, in cooler moments, what is past, often will he find that this one rash act will furnish reflections more than sufficient to embitter his future life. The Christian, through the exercise of meekness and forbearance, prevents the passion from rising; and, in the true spirit of his Master, forgives the injury received. *Being reviled, he blesses; being defamed, he entreats; and prays for those who despitefully use him.* This spirit and this conduct will not pursue and torment him, in his moments of retirement, with bitter reflections, with painful regret, with remorse of conscience; it will spread through his soul, and over his life, the blessings of peace; even the *peace of God which passeth all understanding.*

There are some who, though sufficiently guarded against the more violent passions, are yet subject to constant uneasiness and disquietude from the ordinary occurrences of every day. If all the details of domestic arrangements are not performed with mathematical exactness; if the furniture is not rubbed in a particular way; if the fuel is not laid on the fire according to a precise rule—a rule, too, known only to themselves; if one corner of the table-cloth is but an eighth of an inch lower than the other, &c. &c., they complain, they are vexed, they are unhappy. Now, for this fretful, dissatisfied temper, the gospel offers a sovereign remedy. As the Christian advances in the divine life, he is delivered from this troop of *little foxes*, which spoil the vines of their tender grapes; from that habitual impatience with trifles, which, though it does not expose him to reproach from the world or censure from the church, yet unfits him for devotion, and retards his progress in holiness. Not that the Christian is less observant, or less attentive to neatness and order in his arrangements than others, but he cannot sacrifice his peace of mind on account of such minute irregularities; he has risen above that region in the moral atmosphere where such things produce their annoyance. The most effectual way to deliver the mind from the vexation of trifling cares is to bring it under the influence of those which are truly important. These things, compared with the more weighty concerns even of this world, deserve but little attention; and in presence of the grand objects of eternity, with which the Christian's mind is deeply impressed, and from which he derives his chief happiness, they lose their power to annoy. If your friends were aiding your escape from a house on fire, you would not complain, provided your escape and your safety were secured, though they did not observe all the little punctilios of politeness in affording that aid. In the absence of the sun, the stars are visible; but no sooner does he appear than they shrink from observation, and are seen no more. The Christian is *doing a great work*, he cannot come down to these minute inquiries; he is running a race for a prize of infinite value, he cannot stop to complain of the slight inequalities of the path.

It is, therefore, a *blessing* to any man to be *turned from his iniquity;* to be delivered from those violent and sinful passions which fill his bosom with anxiety and tumult; and to have produced in their stead, those pious affections, those friendly and social feelings which bring with them peace and joy to his own breast. At the same time, while harmony reigns in his own mind, having become a *new creature*, having *put on Christ*, he is disposed to be more kind and affectionate to his friends, and more useful to the church, to society, and to the world. The transformation of a sinful character into the meekness and lowliness of the Saviour's image is a two-fold blessing to society. It is turning a source of disquietude and misery, into a source of peace and happiness; a fountain of bitter, poisonous, and dangerous water, into a salutary, healthful, and refreshing stream; it is changing an enemy into a kind and valuable friend. This truth was never more clearly nor more forcibly exemplified than in the case of Saul of Tarsus. He was one of the most fearful enemies the infant church had to dread. His very name was a terror to the disciples; for he *breathed out threatening and slaughter against* them. Merely to have been delivered from such an enemy, would have been a great blessing:

but to have this same enemy, with all his mighty powers of mind, with all his learning, with all his characteristic ardour and zeal, turned into a decided and active friend; into one of the most intrepid advocates, one of the most laborious, persevering, and successful preachers the church ever had, was a blessing still greater, and called for still more devout and thankful acknowledgments. It is not strange, therefore, that when the disciples heard that he was now *preaching the faith which once he destroyed*, that they *glorified God in him*. This, in a greater or less degree, is the effect of every instance of real conversion by the word and the Spirit of God.

Look at the proud man, whose brow is continually arched with arrogance, whose step and movement are indications of the haughty spirit that reigns within; would you expect this man to be a tender and affectionate husband, or father, or brother? Would you not rather expect that in the bosom of his family, removed from the restraint of public observation, that he will be distant, unfeeling, and morose; impatient, if his wants are not attended to before they are known; expecting every member of his family to gratify his wishes without the satisfaction of knowing that he was pleased with their attention? Would you expect him to perform those offices of kindness, little, indeed, when separately considered, but returning so frequently as to make up a large amount of domestic happiness? Would you expect to see him seeking out the poor, the suffering, and distressed, and ministering to their comfort and relief? No: the incongruity of his spirit to these offices of kindness, utterly forbids the expectation. To perform these offices; to occupy this province of usefulness, you naturally look to the man who is *clothed with humility.* You as naturally expect that this *lowliness of mind* is associated with that benevolence and meekness, with that gentleness and charity which are features of the same character; and that the man possessing this spirit will sweeten the scenes of domestic life with his good will, his kindness, and condescension, and that he will take pleasure in searching out and relieving the poor and the afflicted, as you expect the proud man to be a petty, unfeeling tyrant at home, and to leave the poor and distressed in their unpitied suffering. Think of all the relations of life and of society; of father, of husband, of brother, of friend, of neighbour, of teacher, of magistrate, of legislator, of judge, of chief ruler; and is it not more than probable, that if in other respects they are equal, in talents, in learning, in wealth, every human being, capable of perceiving the difference, would prefer the man of sincere humility to the proud man in either of these relations?

Would you see the difference exemplified, as it regards the happiness of mankind, between the spirit of ambition, and those desires for worldly distinctions which are graduated by the scale of truth? Permit us, for this purpose, again to bring before you, those two men, of all others the most distinguished on the theatre of modern times—Bonaparte and Washington. There is reason to believe that Bonaparte, when he commenced his public career, had no intention of reaching the throne of France. All that he then hoped to attain, in all probability, was the reputation of an accomplished general. But, as he advanced, success fed and increased his ambition, till at length it prompted him to seize the sceptre, which he perceived was held by a feeble and unsteady hand. Reaching this elevated theatre, his ambition receives a new and powerful impulse from beholding the new rivals and competitors, with whom he is surrounded, in the neighbouring sovereigns of Europe. These must be equalled, then excelled, and then humbled. The generals who were once his rivals are now his subordinate agents. His fame and his dominion are now to be extended. For this purpose the lives of hundreds and thousands were sacrificed. He alleged, it is true, other reasons for his measures; his professed object was to give freedom to Europe; but the millions who were subjugated to his power felt the iron hand of despotism. The world and posterity will testify that the incalculable miseries which marked his progress were chiefly if not solely to gratify his boundless ambition. Washington was called, by the voice of his country, to one of the most difficult, arduous, and important stations to which it was possible for that country to call him. After spending successive years of toil and privation and peril in that station, he neither asked nor would receive the smallest compensation for his services. He was instrumental in obtaining for his country the blessings of civil and religious liberty; the invaluable inheritance of every American: and may kind Providence secure this inheritance to our posterity till the last moment of time! This object being accomplished, he leaves the public theatre on which he had acted so conspicuous a part, and returns to his beloved retirement, there to enjoy the only reward which his heart desired, the blessings of peace with his fellow-citizens. Which of these was the most useful to mankind? The one convulsed all Europe, and filled whole empires with tumult, with desolation, with mourning, with sorrow, with death: the other, at the call of his country cheerfully shared in the fatigues and the hazards of war; and in connection with his illustrious companions, in the senate and in the field, procured for his beloved country independence and freedom—blessings which we to this hour enjoy. The difference is too striking to escape observation, and the conclusion too obvious to admit the least doubt.

SECTION IV.

Meekness, Forbearance, Kindness, &c., promote Human Happiness.

WE speak of the man who is a Christian, not merely by assuming the name, and making the profession, but who is such in reality; whose character is forming by the word and Spirit of God, to greater and greater degrees of resemblance to the character of Christ. Surround this man with the provocations and trials which excite the anger, resentment, impatience, fretfulness, &c., of others; and we maintain that he will contribute to the peace and happiness of society in a much greater degree, in consequence of possessing this character, than others in similar circumstances would do. What is the most plausible reason assigned for resenting an insult and avenging an injury? It is to prevent a repetition of the offence. If you tamely submit, it is alleged, you draw on yourself the reproach of cowardice; you invite aggression by declaring that you may be insulted with impunity. Show yourself a man of spirit; resent the injuries you receive, and they will not be repeated. This is the way, this is the language, and this is the spirit of the world. The Bible teaches a different method, holds a different language, and infuses into the Christian a different spirit. The question is, which of them is most conducive to the happiness of man. Has cowardice a more natural connection with meekness, forbearance, and the forgiveness of injuries than it has with those passions which inflict these injuries? If courage be, as some suppose it, in part at least, a natural quality, or constitutional trait of character, then, the want of is not criminal, any more than the want of bodily strength. Has the Christian no other way of manifesting his magnanimity than by the indulgence of anger, malice, and resentment, and by inflicting punishment on those who displease him? Does it not display more true courage and fortitude to subdue these turbulent passions, and maintain meekness and tranquillity of mind, under those provocations, which, in the opinion of the world, will justify resentment and revenge? Is it not a much more decisive proof of pusillanimity and cowardice to insult a man when it is known that he, by his religious principle, is restrained from resistance, than it is, from the heart to forgive the insult? It is the mark of a mean, pitiful soul to vent its wrath on the unresisting; but it is a noble achievement, a mark of real fortitude, to conquer those passions which would prompt to retaliation. In the opinion of the world, it is much more difficult to exercise forbearance, and to forgive an injury, than it is to indulge resentment and to seek revenge. According to this opinion there is more magnanimity displayed in forgiving an injury, than in revenging it. *He that is slow to anger, is better than the mighty; and he that ruleth his spirit, than he that taketh a city.* We recommend on this subject, an excellent sermon of Dr. Witherspoon on *Christian Magnanimity.*

But let us suppose that you act on the principles of the world; when you are reviled, that you revile again; when you are abused, that you return the abuse with interest; when threatened, with a louder and more angry tone you threaten in return; with a spirit corresponding with your words, you curse those who curse you; that to the utmost of your power you exert yourself to overcome evil with evil, to injure those who injure you, whether it be in character, in property, or in person. Now, it is possible, that your language, in this terrible conflict may be so much more abusive, reproachful, bitter, and wounding to the feelings, than that of your antagonist; and that your resentment and your strength may be so much greater than his, that you inflict a greater injury on him than he can on you; that he may be induced, from the principle of mere selfishness, to desist, and not to attack *you* again. But unless you surpass him in your reviling, your threatening, your cursing, your rage, and the punishment you inflict, this purpose will not be answered; he will be just as likely to return on you again, as he will on any other person; and indeed more so: for he will be more gratified with his triumph over one who makes some resistance, than over one who makes none; this will be a more decisive proof of his superiority in those qualities on account of which he values himself. Unless therefore, you can make him afraid of your abuse, your resentment, and your power, you do not secure your safety from future insults. And if you should excite his fear, and thus secure your own safety, you leave him with all his malevolence to attack others who may not possess your talents for reviling and for injury. Your resentment has not the slightest tendency to extinguish his passions, but rather to increase them. He will, therefore, most probably seek to gratify that revenge which your opposition has excited on those who cannot make the same resistance.

Besides; the very first anger that flashes from your eye, the first resentful word you utter, will increase his anger, and his language will be more provoking; this will increase, and justify your resentment on the same principle on which the first feeling of this nature is justified. *As coals are to burning coals, and wood to fire; so is a contentious man to kindle strife. Grievous words stir up anger. A wrathful man stirreth up strife.* One word brings on another; and each one more bitter, more provoking than the preceding. Thus passion increases, till two rational beings are turned into perfect furies. *Behold, how great a matter a little fire kindleth!* How small was the beginning of this tremendous conflict of angry and revengeful passions! And is it possible this is the way, and this the spirit best calculated to promote the happiness of man? Is it possible that a Christian, under any circumstances, can act this part, and cherish these feelings? As soon might we suppose that the innocent dove should dart on its prey with all the unfeeling rapine of the eagle or the hawk; that the meek and harmless lamb should roam through the forest with the rage and fierceness of the hungry lion or the tiger.

Let us suppose, then, that you possess the Christian character; and that you are conscientiously governed by the principles of the Bible. You will then *follow peace with all men. If it be possible, as much as lieth in you,* you will *live peaceably with all men;* you will *follow after the things which make for peace;* you will so *bridle the tongue* as not to *offend in word.* You will not, with expressions, indeed, of regret, but with secret pleasure, take up and circulate a reproach against your neighbour, merely because you can give the author from whom you received it. No person who undertakes the fruitless task of tracing back to its author, some vague, though scandalous report, will find you a link in the chain, along which it has been communicated. You will be no *tale-bearer:* you will not cherish that censorious spirit which would lead you to *back-bitings, whisperings*, against those, whom decency and a regard to public opinion restrain you from defaming more openly. No secret ill-will, envy, or jealousy, will permit you to be gratified in hearing from others that calumny and detraction of your neighbour's character, which motives of selfish policy prevent you from uttering yourself. Your piety will be of that sound, scriptural character which will give no just cause of offence to any human being. Your zeal will be guarded by prudence, by that wisdom that cometh down from above. Your private devotion will be without any thing, intended and understood by others, as a signal to give information of its performance. When called to act before others, you will not display that vain ostentation which is gratified with public observation. If you give reproof, it will not be with that harsh and unfeeling language, better calculated to irritate than to soften and reform; but with that mildness and gentleness which will give weight and even keenness to the reproof. If you give advice on any subject, it will not be with a dogmatizing, dictating spirit, but with that kindness and affection which will be calculated to gain admittance to the heart, and to persuade. Cherishing this spirit, and pursuing this deportment, those who might be disposed to calumniate or injure you, *shall not find any occasion against you, except,* like Daniel, *they find it against you concerning the law of your God.* Your example may reproach and condemn those who are determined to live in sin; your reproof, however, wisely and tenderly given, may irritate those who will not reform. To silence, if possible, the voice of an accusing conscience, and to justify their perseverance in sin, they may say all manner of evil against you; they may revile you for righteousness' sake; but they cannot, in our highly favoured country, persecute you on account of religion; that is, as we understand it, they cannot prosecute you at the civil law. But however pious and friendly may be your disposition, however harmless may be your life, we will not affirm that you will not, on other accounts than religion, meet with trials, and provocation, and injuries from the sinful passions of men. We do think, however, that such a life will secure you, in a great measure, from these trials and provocations. In many cases, he who is considered the aggressor, has some cause for his anger; we do not mean a justifiable one; for nothing can justify these criminal passions; but some unguarded word or action, which might have been avoided, without sacrificing one religious feeling, or violating one obligation; something which disturbs and irritates a mind uninfluenced by the principles of the gospel. God may permit these trials to surround you, for the purpose of calling into exercise, and strengthening, some of the most amiable virtues of the Christian character. It is only under provocation, that meekness and forbearance can be exercised; only when an injury is received, that the spirit of forgiveness can exert its heavenly influence. Such are the views which the Bible gives on this subject. *My brethren,* says the Apostle James, *count it all joy when ye fall into divers temptations:* and again; *blessed is the man that endureth temptation.* The word *temptation* includes the trials to which we refer. They are *divers,* that they may furnish occasion for the exercise of every principle of the Christian character; they are to be *endured;* that is, their tendency to excite any degree of criminal passion, or to lead from the path of duty, must be resisted and overcome by those very principles, which they are intended to call into exercise and strengthen. When the presence of suffering is felt, then, *patience is to have her perfect work;* when provocation is offered, then, meekness and forbearance are called for; when an injury is received, then, forgiveness is to be exercised. It is a cause of blessedness and joy, when these trials, without leading to sin, are the means of advancing towards perfection these pious and amiable dispositions of the heart. It is in connection with this very subject, that the apostle gives those wise and salutary exhortations.—*Let every man be slow to speak, slow to wrath. Wherefore lay apart all filthiness and superfluity of naughtiness, and receive with meekness the ingrafted word, which is able to save your souls.* In the midst of these revilings, and calumnies, and injuries, from a wicked world, you will have this very great advantage: the consciousness of innocence for your support. With confidence you can commit yourself to *Him who judgeth righteously*, and feel the assurance that in his sight, you are not culpable. You need not adopt the finesse of displaying your anger and resentment, as proof that you are unjustly assailed; for this, at best, is but equivocal proof of the fact. When provocation is given, honestly obey the principles of the Bible, be a *doer of the word;* and we maintain, that you will not only preserve the peace of your own mind, but you will very much contribute to the happiness of society. We maintain this point on the authority of the Bible itself; and, if we mistake not, it is confirmed by experience and observation. We have never known an instance, in which the precepts of the Bible were faithfully exemplified, that was not followed by the happiest consequences. All those contentions, which often leave animosities seated in the hearts of two numerous parties, and not unfrequently lead to blood and to murder, commence with but a slight degree of anger, which, if proper measures were pursued, would be quite manageable. Words are generally the first indication of the rising passion within, with these the first onset is made. Then is the very time to try the utility and power of the precepts of the Bible, and test the truth of its declarations. *A soft answer turneth away wrath*, is one of these declarations. If you have done wrong, have given any cause of offence, make a suitable apology; and if your aggressor be a man of generous spirit, this will satisfy him. If you are conscious of innocence, shielded with meekness, forbear to use language intended or calculated to irritate and provoke; let your reply be mild and conciliating. No fuel being furnished to the flame, it will most probably subside. Perceiving no signs of anger or resentment, he will pause, his thoughts will take a different direction, and his wrath will be turned away. If, however, it should be otherwise, if his own words should increase his anger; if, having uttered one provoking word, he should think another still more abusive necessary to justify the first; if he should exhaust the whole vocabulary of vituperation and cursing; and if he still meets with nothing but mildness, he will see that he is wasting his wrath for no purpose; he will be disappointed in perceiving that you are not irritated, that you do not feel his attack, will see that he is exposing himself, and shame will suppress his resentment. *A soft tongue breaketh the bone.* This will be making a fair experiment on the principles of the Bible; and we venture to affirm, that every experiment of this kind will prove the powerful tendency of these principles to preserve the peace and promote the happiness of society. This anger, in the very commencement, will most probably be suppressed by your mildness; but if, without resistance from you, it should rage on till it exhausts itself, he will much sooner feel disposed to be reconciled to you; and if his nature does not bear the

THE INFLUENCE OF THE BIBLE. 161

stamp of the most extreme baseness, such will be his feelings of disappointment and shame, that he will be less likely to attack you a second time, than if you had felt and manifested a spirit of resentment.

Again: *If thine enemy hunger, feed him; if he thirst, give him drink; for in so doing thou shalt heap coals of fire on his head: Be not overcome of evil, but overcome evil with good.* This implies more than mere forbearance and mildness; it requires the exercise of benevolence, doing good to him who has injured, or who intends to injure you. *Love your enemies*—The love of complacency you cannot cherish towards any man whose character, in your opinion, is not worthy of it; but the love of benevolence you can, and ought to feel towards all men, even your bitterest enemy. If he is in distress or affliction, comfort and relieve him, and cheerfully embrace every opportunity of doing him good; not merely once or twice, but as often as the opportunity may offer. This active benevolence, this persevering kindness, will subdue his opposition, will soften his heart, and awaken friendly feelings towards you. Though he should not acknowledge it, yet, if you can make him *feel* that you have done him good, conscious that he does not deserve it, this very feeling will destroy his enmity, as certainly as metal will melt in the midst of burning coals. Until this feeling is produced in the heart of your enemy, the object is not accomplished;

hence you must not *grow weary in well doing;* in the midst of discouragements you must persevere in kindness. It is not sufficient merely to cast the metal into the fire—the degree of heat, and the length of time, must be sufficient to answer the purpose. One kind of metal will melt with a less degree of heat, and in a shorter time than another. If your kindness fails to soften your enemy and change him into a friend, it is for want of perseverance, or for want of catching the occasion most favourable to success. There are different degrees of enmity; one degree will be overcome by that kindness which will produce but little effect on another. Some hearts are more easily touched with kindness than others. Under certain circumstances, and after a certain train of thought, your enemy may spurn your kindness; but let the circumstances in which he is placed and the state of his mind be different, and the effect will be different. Therefore, do not despair; *in due season you shall reap, if you faint not.* You shall, sooner or later, see your enemy overcome by your goodness, changed into a friend, and willing to acknowledge your kindness. If the metal does not melt in a given time, let it remain still longer; if one degree of heat is insufficient, increase that degree, and the purpose will be answered. Overcome evil with good: this exhortation surely does not require you to do what is impossible, but what is practicable by persevering in the use of those means calculated to answer the purpose. If *seven* instances of kindness are not successful, you are not to doubt the truth of the gospel, and give up the task as entirely hopeless: you are to try the force of *seventy times seven;* each instance rendered with more cordiality, if possible, than the preceding. Cherish the firm conviction that in due time the purpose will be accomplished, that the Lord shall reward you with success; your enemy will, at length, feel and acknowledge that you have done him good; and it is under the influence of this feeling that his enmity begins to melt, and that friendly dispositions towards you arise in his heart. Thus you will gain a brother, perhaps, save a soul from death, and prevent a multitude of sins, preserve peace and harmony when discord and strife would have taken place, and probably have been transmitted to future generations.

You are not to allege, as an excuse for your neglect or want of perseverance, that the duty is difficult. You are not to sit in judgment on the wisdom and propriety of the divine precepts, cast off the authority of your moral governor, and assume the right of prescribing for yourself that service which he ought to accept. If you claim this right, you must grant it to others, and thus it will be made to cover the neglect of every duty. You may allege that it is difficult to forgive and do good to an enemy who has injured you; that it is much easier to resent and retaliate. Another may allege with equal truth, that prayer, *with the spirit and with the understanding*, is very difficult to him; another, that the proper observance of the Sabbath is extremely irksome to him: will this be a sufficient excuse for the neglect of these important duties? No more in either of these cases than it will in your own. Would you extend the same right to the citizens of the state? Your neighbour is indolent, he cannot labour, *to beg he is ashamed*, he finds it difficult to be honest and to abstain from stealing your property. Will you excuse him on this ground? If not, excuse not yourself by the same reason for neglecting a duty on which the peace and happiness of society so much depend. In the case of your neighbour, this excuse would be the confession of his own guilt, and proof that he was not a good citizen. So will it be in your own case: a confession that your faith in the word of God is weak, and that you possess but little of the spirit of your divine Saviour, whom you profess to love, and whose example you have publicly and solemnly pledged yourself to imitate. If you possessed more of that meekness, forbearance, and kindness which characterized the Saviour, this difficulty would not be so great. Nor are you to allege that your aggressor has done wrong, and therefore deserves punishment. This is admitted; but at whose hands does he deserve it: will you assume the right of inflicting punishment when it is deserved? This is the prerogative which God most explicitly claims to himself: *Vengeance is mine, I will repay, saith the Lord.* When you undertake to avenge yourself, surely you cannot reflect on all the consequences. The wilful transgression of his law is bold and impious rebellion against him; by what name shall we call it, then, to arrogate and presume to exercise one of the sacred and awful perfections of God? Besides, you not only teach God, but you do virtually pray to him that he would treat you as you do those who offend or injure you. Every degree of anger and resentment which you feel—every provoking word you utter— every effort you make to injure your adversary, is an appeal to God that he would visit you; not with the pardon of sin, according to his tender mercy, but in justice, according to the guilt of your offences against him. It is from the assurance that God will execute justice that your duty is inferred —*I will repay; therefore, if thine enemy hunger, feed him, &c.* If the Sovereign Judge had not pledged himself to do justice, this duty would not be so forcibly and so clearly enjoined. This pledge from God takes away from you the plea that your enemy deserves punishment. The world, indeed, will justify your resentment and your retaliation; but the world is ignorant of the principles by which, as a Christian, you are governed. *The world knoweth us not.* The spirit and principles of the Christian character are foolishness to the natural man; *neither can he know them, because* they are spiritually discerned. He that is spiritual discerneth all things, yet he himself is discerned of no man. You are not to be *conformed to this world* in its spirit, its principles, or its practice. You are not to reject the declarations of the Bible as if their truth and their tendency were doubtful, and in their place adopt the maxims and spirit of an ignorant and wicked world. You are to cherish the spirit and imitate the example of Christ, who prayed for the pardon of those enemies who nailed him to the cross.

There is a collateral view of the subject which enforces this duty and confirms the hope that your kindness will transform your enemy into a friend; it is the method of the gospel in bringing sinners to God; they are softened, and subdued, and changed by kindness. Every human being, by nature, feels towards God an enmity which is deep-rooted, active, and persevering. This opposition never has been and never will be subdued by any degree of terror which sinners can be made to feel. It is melted away by the influence of sovereign grace; and especially by that astonishing instance of unmerited goodness and infinite mercy, the pardon of sin. The very moment the hope of pardon is cherished, that moment this enmity dies, to revive no more as a dominant principle in the heart, and love to God ascends the throne in its place. Enemies are changed into friends, not by the terrors of the law, nor by the sword of justice, but by the loving-kindness displayed through the cross of Christ. Now if we were not creatures and bound to obey our Sovereign, if we really desired to be most useful to mankind, we would most successfully adopt that method which the wisdom of God has devised, and which he employs in converting sinners to himself, in transforming determined enemies into sincere and cordial friends. If God, who is better acquainted with the nature of men than we are, has appointed this method, and uniformly employs the instrumentality of kindness in changing his enemies into friends, we may confidently hope for success on the same plan, and by the same means.

Why, it may be asked, do we not see and feel more of the blessed and happy effects of these principles of the Christian religion? One reason is, there are thousands who profess to be Christians, who are not such in reality; they are, in fact, governed by the principles of the world. They have a name that they live, but are dead; they have the form of godliness, but feel not its renovating power. They do not *bridle the tongue* from backbiting, from slander, from malicious censure and reproach, and therefore *their religion is vain ;* they do not possess the *spirit of Christ*, which is a spirit of meekness, forbearance, forgiveness, and charity; but, especially when provoked, they manifest a spirit of anger, hatred, malice, and revenge; therefore, we are assured they *are none of his*.

It is most unreasonable to look for the effects of a principle where that principle does not exist. *Do men gather grapes of thorns, or figs of thistles?* No more are we to expect the happy effects of the Bible from those, who, whatever they may profess, are governed by enmity of heart against the spirituality, the purity, and authority of that holy book. There is another reason, which cannot be mentioned without shame and sorrow; that is, the criminal deficiencies and the negligence of Christians. They sometimes feel a want of entire confidence in the truth of the divine declarations regarding this subject; they hesitate whether it would not be better to take the work of vengeance into their own hands. God has promised, indeed, that he will repay; but whether he will do it at the time, and in the manner, and to that degree, which they conceive he ought, is rather doubtful; and although they have his solemn promise that he will do justice in the case, yet a secret fear, which they would not profess, and which they would willingly conceal from their own view, lest he should fail, prompts them to undertake it themselves. Hence, although they are Christians, yet through unbelief lurking in the heart, they do not exemplify their own principles, which are set aside in the present case, and the spirit and principles of the world, as better calculated to answer the purpose, are adopted. In this state of mind, they feel and reason and act as men of the world would do in similar circumstances. There is sometimes a distrust respecting the success of their forbearance and kindness in disarming an enemy of his hostile feelings, and awakening in his bosom those of a friendly character. They will allege that his disposition is too harsh and unfeeling, his resentment too implacable, and his hatred too inveterate to be softened by their kindness. Thus the motive which should urge them forward in persevering efforts is weakened through this secret unbelief, and the case is given up as hopeless. If the husbandman should suffer his mind to be disquieted with doubts and fears respecting the success of his labours, and therefore decline these labours altogether, his doubts and his conduct would be considered both unreasonable and criminal; not less so are Christians, who, through groundless fears, neglect these pious and benevolent exertions. The mere possibility that their efforts may fail, is not an excuse for their declining to make them; they are faithfully to discharge their duty, and leave the event to *God who giveth the increase.* Christians are chargeable with criminal neglect, in not *keeping the heart with all diligence,* at the moment when provocation is offered. It is not their intention to suffer any violent anger to agitate their bosom; but before they are aware, some unhallowed feeling is excited, under the influence of which they speak, not the language of meekness and conciliation, but unguardedly. This provokes their aggressor still more; and they are imperceptibly led to a degree of passion, which, instead of recommending, brings a reproach on their profession, and, in moments of cool reflection, becomes to themselves a source of bitter regret. Good will it be for them, if this regret shall make them more watchful in future; better far, however, had it been, if by watchfulness and prayer they had prevented the cause of this reproach and this regret. All this, however, admitted, it does not in the least affect our position; that the Bible has a direct and powerful tendency, by reforming the heart, to promote the happiness of man; and we do strenuously contend that in all cases this will be the result of its operation. We repeat, that when its principles do not operate, we cannot expect to see their effects. Let Christians guard against the shadow of doubt or distrust respecting the declarations, and cheerfully obey the precepts relating to the duties now under consideration; by watchfulness and prayer, especially when provocation is offered, let them prevent the slightest degree of anger; and they will remove this cause of sorrow and reproach, and support this conclusion by testimony which may bid defiance even to scepticism itself.

Experiment is the best, indeed, the only way to try the tendency of any system or principle; that is, to view it in full and complete operation; and we contend that so far as the experiment has been made, on the principles of the Bible, the result does triumphantly support our conclusion. Let the experiment be more general, and this proof will be more abundant and more undeniable. The voice of inspiration, if we are not mistaken in its meaning, justifies the firm belief, that this earth shall not meet its final doom; that these heavens shall not be rolled together as a scroll, or pass away with a great noise, till an experiment shall be made on a more general scale than has ever yet been witnessed; from which, proof in support of the point for which we contend will be furnished, not less convincing than that derived from mathematical demonstration. Cast forward the eye of faith and hope to that state of the church and of the world, when the sublime and glowing figures of prophetic vision shall be verified; when the life-giving power of the gospel shall destroy the wicked and turbulent passions of men, and awaken in the heart supreme, sincere, and ardent love to God and man; when war and bloodshed will no longer desolate the earth; when anger, malice, and resentment shall no longer corrode the breast, nor disturb the harmony of neighbours, of friends, of brethren; when peace and happiness shall bless this poor, miserable, and sinful world in a degree which has never been experienced since Adam was driven out of Paradise. The prophet, after shadowing forth the joyous harmony of that day by the most significant emblems of peace, closes the account with this summary declaration; *They shall not hurt nor destroy in all my holy mountain;* and then, not leaving us to mere conjecture on the subject, points out the cause of all this blessedness:

For the earth shall be full of the knowledge of the Lord, as the waters cover the sea. The waters of the ocean touch and cover every inch which is below the level of their surface; in like manner, at that time, will every neighbourhood and every family be touched and influenced by the Bible. All the miseries under which the world is now groaning, and from which it will then be relieved; all the peace and happiness which shall then prevail, will be the powerful and genuine effect of the gospel. That gospel is the same now that it will be then. Not another doctrine, not another precept, not another promise or invitation will be added, as the means of producing these glorious and happy effects. The very doctrines, precepts, and promises with which we are favoured, will be effectual for this purpose. The proof derived from an experiment yet to be made, provided we know with certainty the result of the experiment, is the same with that furnished by an experiment actually made. Immutable truth, then declares what will be the result of this grand experiment; that it will fill the earth with friendship, and harmony, and peace, and joy. The effects of the gospel, at that day, and those which it is now, and ever has been producing, differ only in degree, not in kind: of course, it follows, that in proportion to the degree of power which it exerts on the heart and on the conduct of men, it is now, and ever has been, producing the very same effects; and that the world is now so much the less miserable and so much the more happy in exact proportion to its saving and transforming power. Diminish this power, and you increase the sufferings of this life; increase this power, and you increase the happiness of man.

SECTION V.

The Gospel furnishes Support in Affliction—Influence of Faith, Hope, and Love.

After all the happy effects which the gospel is calculated to produce, and is actually producing, there will be numberless afflictions from which the Christian cannot escape; it remains, then, to point out the strong consolation, the powerful support, which the Bible furnishes to him, under the pressure of these sufferings. To mention these afflictions in detail is unnecessary, if it were practicable. The Christian is as liable to epidemical diseases, to losses and disappointments in his property as others are. At least, he is liable to them in some degree; though we are inclined to believe, not quite as much as others; for we think it probable that a life of intemperance and debauchery will predispose the system to disease, more than sobriety and temperance; and that industry, economy, and prudence will guard, in some measure, against those losses and disappointments. He is liable to suffer through his friends; and the valley and shadow of death is before him, which he cannot escape. Besides all these, he meets with trials which are peculiar to the Christian, from the prevalence of sin and temptation in the world. In the midst of all these sufferings the gospel brings him consolation and support which no impenitent sinner can receive. He is not indebted to a mere effort of his imagination for this support, —it arises from the character which he possesses, from the relation he sustains to God and the Saviour, from his faith, his hope, and the devout affections of his heart. These are the means employed by the *Father of mercies* in bearing up his people in the midst of their sufferings. Divest the Christian of this character, dissolve this relation, extinguish these affections, and you cut him off from the source of his comfort, and leave him weak and disconsolate as other men.

View the Christian in the midst of his sufferings, and mark the fortitude with which he endures the most exquisite pain, and the patience and meek submission with which he resigns himself to the will of his heavenly Father. His support is not the sullen, rebellious insensibility of the stoic; he feels and acknowledges the pain which he suffers. He is not so absurd as to deny the difference between pleasure and pain; nor so impious as to deny that the hand of God can afflict him. Under every kind and degree of suffering his faith brings him real and substantial support. This, from the constitution of the human mind, and from the nature of this faith, will be the result of its exercise. If, during the pressure of affliction, the mind dwells chiefly on the pain and distress which are felt; on the pleasures which he once enjoyed, and of which he is now deprived; on the freedom from pain and the peaceful enjoyment of others; and above all, if he can see no good purpose to be answered by his sufferings, the mind will become dispirited and faint, and the pressure of affliction will become heavier and less tolerable; every recollection of the past, every view of present circumstances and future prospects, increases the gloom and despondency under which he is sinking. The Christian is not left *comfortless* in his affliction. His faith furnishes him with materials of thought so deeply interesting and so pleasing as to draw off his attention from the present affliction, and fix it chiefly on objects which prevent despondency, and strengthen, animate, cheer, and support the mind. He believes most firmly that his afflictions, heavy and complicated as they may be, *come not forth of the dust, neither doth his trouble spring out of the ground;* that his afflictions are not the result of accident or of chance, but sent by his heavenly Father to work for his good; that the time, the degree, and all other circumstances relating to them, are determined and regulated by infinite wisdom and goodness; that they are intended to deliver him from the power of remaining sin, detach him more effectually from this world, which is delusive, ensnaring and dangerous; to increase his confidence in God, and render more precious to his heart the Saviour, and that gospel which exhibits the Saviour; to increase his holiness, and thus qualify him in a greater degree for the *joy of his Lord,* for the *inheritance of the saints in light.* While, therefore, he believes that these afflictions are working out for him a *far more exceeding and eternal weight of glory* than he should ever attain without them, he does not faint when rebuked of his Father. Nor does he exhibit that sullen submission arising from mere necessity, because he can neither escape nor remove his afflictions; but resigning himself cheerfully and voluntarily to the will of his God who, he believes, *does not afflict willingly.* His patience preserves him from murmuring, repining, and fretfulness; and he prefers his affliction to any other state, not that it is *for the present joyous, but grievous;* but because it flows from the love and affection of his Friend in heaven, and on account of its tendency to improve his moral character, and thus to fit him for higher degrees of glory and greater measures of happiness during his eternal existence. He feels, in some degree, the Spirit, and may use the language of his Saviour: O my *Father, if it be possible, let this cup pass from me! nevertheless, not as I will, but as thou wilt. O my Father, if this cup may not pass away from me, except I drink it, thy will be done.*

This is the only way in which the mind can be supported under suffering, or comforted under sorrow; that is, by drawing off the thoughts, as much as possible, from the pain which is felt, and fixing them strongly on other objects, which make such impressions on the mind as enable it to bear its sufferings with fortitude. This is the theory according to which the Christian's faith comforts and supports him in the hour of distress. *I had fainted*, said the Psalmist, *unless I had believed to see the goodness of the Lord in the land of the living.* Hence, the exhortation which he offers is the result of his own experience: *Wait on the Lord: be of good courage, and he shall strengthen thine heart: wait, I say, on the Lord.* When Paul, after the fatigues of a perilous voyage, saw the brethren come from Rome to meet him, *he thanked God, and took courage.* The sight, and friendly gratulation of these brethren, furnished a new and pleasing train of thought; these thoughts gave a new spring to his mind, and prepared him with fortitude to bear the present and meet the future trials of his life.

There is a principle belonging to the human mind, called the principle of association. One event, or one object, brings to our recollection and to our thoughts another, with which it is in some way or other connected. It was on this principle, that the presence of these brethren reanimated the apostle's mind with fresh courage. Their presence awoke in his mind a flow of thought, which made him forget the perils of his past life, and enabled him to meet, with unyielding firmness, the trials which awaited him in future. Here are the disciples of that Saviour in whose cause he was engaged, to whom he was under infinite obligations, for whom he had suffered much, and was willing to suffer the loss of all things; here are those who will sympathize with him, and pray for him, and comfort him; here are the fruits of that gospel of which he was not ashamed, and which he was ready to preach at Rome also. Faith would naturally carry his thoughts away from this world, and elevate them to heaven, to dwell on all that is cheering and invigorating there; on his Intercessor and Advocate with the Father; on the multitudes already redeemed from this earth, and now surrounding the throne of God; on that crown of glory, which the Lord, the righteous Judge, shall give him at the last day. With those thoughts his soul *grew warm*, as the word (tharsos) signifies. Thus *he was comforted together with them, by the mutual faith both of them and him.* According to the same principle, when he came into Macedonia, he was pressed with troubles from every side; *without, were fightings, within, were fears: nevertheless, God,* he observes, *who comforteth those who are cast down, comforted us by the coming of Titus.* On this principle it is, that faith supports the Christian. Affliction is strongly associated in his mind with other subjects, which of course it brings to his recollection and his thoughts. He is reminded of his sins, on account of which it is sent, and from which it is intended to deliver him. The goodness of God, who directs this affliction for this important purpose, is brought with pleasure and with invigorating power to his thoughts. The sufferings of the present state forcibly impress upon his mind the insufficiency of this world, as a portion for the soul, and remind him of that *better country*, of that *rest which remains for the people of God*, and increase his desire to *depart and be with Christ which is far better.* Yet this desire is united with the spirit of meek submission, which enables him to say: *all the days of my appointed time will I wait till my change come.*

Hope is another ground of support, and source of consolation to the Christian, under all the trials and distresses of this life. This is not a simple affection, but seems to be compounded of desire and expectation. Desire implies that there is something in its object, the possession of which will contribute to our happiness; expectation implies that there are reasons for believing that we shall possess this object. The object of hope is always future; it will, of course, continually carry the mind away from all that is past, and all that is present, to something still before us. This object will, therefore, give the most pleasing, the most animating employment to our thoughts. It is the nature of all affections, to bring their objects frequently to our thoughts. If the object of these affections be good, then this employment of our thoughts will be pleasing and delightful. Now, the object of hope is always something good; for it is an object of desire. The frequency, the interest, and the pleasure, with which it will occupy the mind, will be in proportion to the degree of happiness expected from its possession. If that view of the object which excites our desire be erroneous, if we suppose it to possess qualities, which it really does not; or if those reasons which support our expectation be fallacious and groundless; then, sooner or later, our hope, however pleasing it may have been, must end in the bitterness of disappointment. But if our views of the object be true, if it really possesses the qualities which we suppose it does; and if the reasons on which our expectation is founded be substantial; then, our *hope will be joy and gladness;* the possession of this object, and the increase of our happiness, are certain. Such is the nature of hope in general, whether its object be temporal or eternal, whether it belongs to this world or to the world of spirits.

Now, it is obvious, that all that is interesting in this analysis is embraced in the Christian's hope. God himself, with all his infinite perfections, is the object of this hope. *The Lord will be the hope of Israel: Blessed is the man whose hope the Lord is.* Christ, the divine Redeemer, is the object of it: *The Lord Jesus Christ, which is our hope.* All that is expressed by the terms *eternal life*, is embraced by this hope: *in hope of eternal life which God hath promised.* All, therefore, that is majestic, and sublime, and venerable, and gracious, and merciful, and lovely in the Triune Jehovah; all that is joyful, and glorious, and eternal in the happiness of heaven, is included in the object of this hope. That view of these objects, or that knowledge which excites the Christian's desire, cannot be erroneous; for it is the truth of God himself. Those reasons on which his expectation is founded cannot deceive him; for they are the declarations, the promises of immutable veracity; together with that degree of holiness, or fitness for the enjoyment of these objects, which he has already acquired. These are the *reasons* which he is ready to give for the hope that is in him. This hope, from its very nature, has a powerful tendency to promote this holiness, to increase this fitness, and thus to strengthen the foundation on which it is built. *For every man that hath this hope in him, purifieth himself, even as he,* who is the object of it, *is pure.* This shows the connection which hope has with faith; a connection similar to that of the effect with the cause, or the germ and the stalk with the seed and the root. The true character of God, and the nature of heaven are made known in his word; it is therefore the knowledge and belief of this word which excite that desire which is an essential part of hope. This same truth sanctifies the heart, and contains the promises which support expectation; the other essential part of hope. Hence *faith is the substance of things hoped for,* because it is, *the evidence of things not seen.* He that would blast this hope, must divest Jehovah of his character; he that would shake its foundation, must shake the truth of heaven itself. The Christian, therefore, cannot have faith without hope, nor hope without faith. If he has the support of faith, he has also the *rejoicing of hope.*

This hope is, at all times, and under all circumstances, interesting to the Christian. When surrounded by the smiles of worldly prosperity, these smiles are rendered more cheering by the presence of this hope. But when the sun of prosperity is clouded from his view; when trials perplex him; when distress invades him; when the weight of affliction presses heavily upon him; when every rivulet of earthly comfort is drying up; then is this hope peculiarly interesting; then does he realize the truth of the remark that " hope is the balm of life;" then is this hope *as an anchor to the soul, both sure and steadfast,* because it *entereth into that within the vail;* or, " because fixed into the place within the vail ; that is, into heaven, whither he shall be drawn, by this anchor, as ships are drawn to the place where their anchors are fixed." From the dark gloom with which he is surrounded not one cheering ray of light breaks on his mind. His present circumstances, viewed only in the light which this world can shed on them, suggest none but ideas calculated to depress and overwhelm the mind. The light of faith strengthens and animates him, by showing the connection between these afflictions and his own salvation, and the lovingkindness and goodness of his Father. Hope pours her cordial into his bosom, and revives his spirit with the light of life. Hope at all times leads the mind away from the past and the present to things that are future; and never does the mind stretch forward with more intense eagerness than from those scenes where all is dark and comfortless, and discouraging. The objects of hope are always pleasing and welcome to the thoughts; never more so than now, when every thought from the world is afflictive and dispiriting. His body remains on earth, exposed to suffering; but his thoughts are employed about the objects of hope; and the more he thinks of them, the more desirable and the more consoling do they become. The foundation of this hope is considered, its firmness is tried; and the more closely it is examined, the more solid and immoveable does it appear. While his thoughts are thus employed, his soul is warmed and invigorated with a glow of pious and devout feeling, which, though it may not remove, yet lightens the pressure of affliction. The inconveniences of life, the sufferings and pains of the body afflict and depress the mind just in proportion as they fix the attention and employ the thoughts; just in proportion, therefore, as other objects of a pleasing nature occupy the attention, they will bring comfort and support to the mind. How strong, then, is the consolation which hope brings to the Christian under all the nameless evils and sufferings of this life! No suffering can draw his thoughts away from spiritual objects; of these he will think, on account of these sufferings, with more intense application, and derive from them more consolation and support. He is, therefore, *saved by hope;* saved from murmuring, impatience, and despondency. With all the *full assurance of hope* he anticipates the last hour of his conflict and his sufferings, and his entrance into the joy of his Lord. Compared with this joy, his are *light afflictions;* compared with its eternal duration, they *endure but for a moment.* The hope which brightens the darkest scenes with the cheering light of heaven, which animates and supports him through the trials of life, and enables him to triumph in the hour of death, must be a GOOD HOPE.

Love is another affection, from which the human mind derives no little enjoyment. It is called into exercise by the view of something good, the possession of which would contribute to our happiness. It also presents its object to our thoughts with a frequency and a pleasing interest in proportion to the amiable qualities by which it is excited, and the degree of happiness expected from possession. From the frequency with which its object engages our thoughts, this affection exerts a transforming influence on the mind. This is especially the case when its objects are of our own species. This affection inclines us to construe their whole deportment in the most favourable light. It renders us blind to their defects and their blemishes, and generally suggests an excuse for their faults. It magnifies their virtues, and very much enhances the value of the favours they confer on us. Their presence, their conversation, imparts to the mind a pleasing elasticity, and awakens an exhilarating glow of feeling which is one of the purest earthly joys. When they are absent, past interviews are called up with the fondest recollection, and future meetings are anticipated with all the joyous ardour of hope. We find a pleasure in acting according to their desires, and are ready, with cheerfulness, to make any sacrifice of our own convenience or comfort to promote their happiness. We are delighted to hear their praise from others, and the slightest reproach on their character gives us pain. We are disposed to adopt their sentiments, and imitate their examples; and thus we are very much under their influence, and our happiness and respectability are, in no small degree, placed in their power. If those whom we love are truly virtuous and worthy, our affection for them will raise us in the estimation of the good and the wise, and contribute very much to our happiness in life. But if they are unworthy and vicious, our affections will sink us with them to misery and disgrace. Such are the effects of love; and it is better defined by its effects than by any other method.

When this affection is directed to God and the

Saviour, its tendency to contribute to our happiness and especially to support us under affliction, must be obvious to every one. It is excited by a view of the moral perfections of the divine character; and the more accurate and the more extensive our views of these perfections are, the more ardent, sincere, and delightful will this affection be. These perfections are displayed in the works of creation and providence, but chiefly in the cross of Christ, and in the salvation of sinners. Hence we see the connection of this love with faith, by which we behold these glories revealed in the gospel. The moment we are united to Christ by faith, that moment we have such a view of the infinite goodness and mercy of God as kindles this devout and heavenly affection in our hearts. As our faith increases, our love will increase with it. *We love him, because he first loved us ;* and this is the manifestation of his love towards us, *that he sent his only begotten Son into the world, that we might live through him.*

Consider the direct and powerful effect which this love will have in supporting and comforting the Christian under all the losses and disappointments and sorrows of this life. Is he disappointed in his expectations, and deprived of worldly enjoyments? Love will interpret these dispensations of providence as blessings, because they are part of the designs and works of God. Is he perplexed and annoyed with temptations? This is to try his faith, and prove the sincerity of his attachment to the

Saviour and his cross. Is he brought down by sickness? This, though for the present not joyous, but grievous, is understood as an evidence of fatherly kindness and attention; for *whom the Lord loveth he chasteneth, and scourgeth every son whom he receiveth.* Is he called to weep at the grave of his pious friends? They are *taken away from the evil to come;* they are with Christ, *which is far better* than to remain here. Is he at length called to enter the *valley and shadow of death?* He will *fear no evil;* for that God and Saviour whom he loves *will be with him;* it is the termination of his conflicts and his sorrows; *to die is gain.* Every duty is sweetened; every gloomy, desponding thought is met and repelled; every difficulty and trial is surmounted; every affliction is lightened, and even welcomed; and death itself is stripped of all its terror, and changed into an angel of mercy, by love. This heaven-born affection cheers and supports him through every scene of life, dispels the darkness from the tomb, and sheds its brightest and mildest splendours over all the realities of eternity.

Such is the support and consolation which the Bible affords the Christian, under those afflictions from which he cannot escape; and such is the manner in which this support is derived, and in which the mind is sustained and comforted. Hope and love are excited by objects most worthy of these affections, and most powerfully calculated to call them forth. These affections fill the mind with a cheerful glow of approbation of the character of God, and the dispensations of his providence, under which these sufferings occur. Hope and love, together with that faith from which they spring, and with which they are inseparably connected, are the means by which a gracious God preserves his people from despair, fills them with comfort, and not unfrequently renders them *exceeding joyful in all their tribulation*.

Numerous facts, derived from the history of the human mind, might be adduced to confirm and illustrate this theory. This is the method adopted by the captive Indian, who knows nothing of Christ or of his gospel, when bound to the stake, and doomed to expire under all the protracted tortures which the ingenuity of his enemies can inflict. He cannot render himself insensible; when the flesh and the sinews are torn by inches from the bone, he must feel the most exquisite pain. He does not leave his mind entirely vacant, to resist his sufferings by simple efforts of volition; but by a strong effort of thought, he remembers the heroism and renown of his ancestors, and feels that it now depends on him to maintain and transmit to posterity the invincible firmness and characteristic bravery of his nation, and particularly of his own family. These are the thoughts which fortify his mind; and these are the reasons, on account of which, he defies his enemies, mocks their imbecility, suffers and dies without gratifying them with a single complaint or a single groan.

When the general of an army observes his soldiers advancing with trembling and hesitating steps, dispirited and timid, without the animating influence of hope, influenced by secret apprehensions of the result, shrinking from the contest; he adopts this method to cheer their spirits and invigorate their minds with courage. In his harangue, if he cannot deny the facts, and disprove the reports which have chilled their minds, he labours to divert their thoughts, as much as possible, from these discouraging topics, and fix them on objects pleasing and animating in their nature. His knowledge of the human mind will be displayed by the fitness and tendency of his remarks, to answer this special purpose. If he can gain the direction of their thoughts, he will succeed; he will inspire them with the cheering hope of victory, and with courage and resolution for the contest. But if he cannot gain this direction; if he cannot break the association of their thoughts, with the gloomy subjects which intimidate and depress their spirits, his effort is vain, his labour is lost. Prudence will suggest to him the policy of declining the contest with soldiers already vanquished in their own apprehension.

This is the true theory of persuasion, and shows the powerful and astonishing effects of eloquence on the mind. To persuade, is to present considerations calculated to secure the performance of a particular

act, or the pursuit of a certain course of conduct.
Passions are the great motives to action; these can
be excited, only by fixing the thoughts on objects
calculated to produce this effect. Persuasion implies that there is more or less aversion to the action
or the course proposed; this, again, implies an association of thought with objects which feed this
aversion. This association is to be dissolved, and
this aversion is to be overcome. Other objects are
to be presented to the mind, which will give such a
direction to the thoughts, and awaken such passions
as accord with the ultimate design. This task will
try the power, and skill, and art of the orator.
With this view, he will delight the fancy with the
beauty of his images, and the brilliancy of the dress
in which he clothes his ideas. He will impart to
the most trite and common subjects all the charms
of novelty; and interest his hearers by his action,
by the expression of his countenance, and by the
modulation of his voice. He will prepossess his
hearers in his favour, by modesty and tenderness,
or astonish them with boldness and energy, just as
the progress of feeling seems to require. If he gives
pleasure and delight, it is not because this is his
ultimate object, but that he may dissolve those associations of thought, and efface those feelings which
are unfriendly to his purpose; that he may open
an easy and direct access to the understanding, and
gain a complete control over the thoughts. This
accomplished, his point is gained; he can then

touch those chords of the heart which will vibrate in perfect unison with his design.

If you wish to comfort a friend in distress, this is the method you adopt. You present the cause of grief in some new light, or introduce subjects which have but little connection with this cause, in order to divert the thoughts into a different channel. If you can succeed in this attempt, your purpose will, in some degree, be answered, your friend, by this diversion of thought, will be relieved from the pressure of his sorrow; but if not, you leave your friend as you found him, with mournful pleasure brooding on those subjects which feed his grief, and waste the vigour of his mind. No case, calling for the kind offices of your friendship, requires a more accurate knowledge of the human mind, and the manner in which it is influenced, than this. You can easily admonish your friend not to grieve; but you might as well admonish the wind not to blow, or the waves of the ocean not to roll, unless you furnish the mind with some antidote to sorrow. The propriety of your remarks will depend on your knowledge of the thoughts and feelings of your friend; without this knowledge, your attempt may not only be useless, but even injurious; it may increase the distress which it was intended to assuage. Guided, however, by this knowledge, if the mind of your friend will admit of comfort, you may leave him with the pleasing reflection, that you have been instrumental in dispelling the gloom from his thoughts, and lightening the burden of his heart.

Such is the method according to which the Lord is pleased to comfort and support his people. The subject is thus divested of that mystery, with which, in the view even of some Christians, it is too often surrounded. They seem to possess a vague idea that divine power will support them, independently of the exercise of their own minds. This opinion is as unscriptural as it is unphilosophical. They might as well expect that the *preserver of men* would support the body without daily bread, as that he will support the mind in distress, without the exercise of faith, and hope, and love, and other devout affections of the heart. Divine power, employed in this way, and for this purpose, would be miraculous; as was the power which preserved the three children in the fiery furnace. If there is a single passage of scripture, which seems to justify this opinion, it is because that passage is not correctly understood, or is perverted. *My grace is sufficient for thee*, is a precious promise, which has borne up, as it did Paul, many a Christian through scenes of the deepest affliction, and enabled him to *take pleasure in infirmities, in reproaches, in necessities, in persecutions, in distresses for Christ's sake.* Now, if any should content themselves with a vague impression that *grace* is a distinct perfection or attribute of the divine character; and that this supposed perfection will be exerted in some mysterious and miraculous way for their support, they will, through their ignorance of the promise, deprive themselves of all the consolation which it was intended to afford. But if by *grace* they understand unmerited favour, they will receive the truth, that God will support them, will measure his kindness to them, not according to what they deserve for their sins, but according to his own good pleasure and sovereign mercy. Faith, and hope, and love, are the work and the gift of God. If he supports and comforts the Christian by means of the exercises of his own mind, it is as certainly his work, and his favour, as if the same effects were produced by immediate and direct agency. No man, therefore, let his profession be what it may, let the exercise of his mind be what it may, who is not a sound Bible Christian, can enjoy that support and consolation which God bestows on his chosen people; and no man, who is such a Christian, can, in proportion to his faith, be without this support. If Christians would read and study the Bible with more frequency, and with more prayerful attention, their knowledge would be more extensive, and more accurate; their faith would be stronger, and more practical; their hope would be firmer; their love would be more ardent and sincere; their life would be more useful to the church, and to the world; their support under afflictions would be more abundant; and their joy and their glory, throughout their eternal existence, would be greater.

SECTION VI.

The Religion of the Bible, the true Happiness of Man.

THE most accurate analysis of human happiness will confirm the truth of the Bible; and particularly of this declaration; *godliness is profitable unto all things, having promise of the life that now is, and of that which is to come.* This happiness is not simple in its nature, but very complex; depending on a variety of circumstances, and derived from a great variety of sources. Pleasure is either animal, or intellectual, or moral, or spiritual. These are distinct sources of enjoyment, which rise above each other in importance and refinement, in the order in which they are here stated. Of these, animal pleasures are the lowest; these we enjoy in common with the brutes. They arise from the conveniences of life, and from the gratification of those propensities and appetites which are peculiar to animal nature. Intellectual pleasure is derived from the exercise and improvement of the mind in the acquisition of knowledge, in the cultivation of arts and science. Here man leaves the level of the brutes, and is elevated to a sphere of enjoyment to which they can never rise. Moral pleasure is derived from the exercise of the moral virtues: truth, justice, honesty, &c.; and from the social affections: benevolence, sympathy, friendship, generosity, &c.; and from those affections which grow out of the conjugal, parental, filial, and fraternal relations. Spiritual pleasure arises from the knowledge and belief of the Bible; and from those pious affections which the Bible, through the agency of the Holy Spirit, excites in the heart: meekness, humility, love, hope, gratitude, &c. This last is peculiar to the Christian. The others, animal, intellectual, and moral, may be enjoyed by those who never do, and never can taste those joys which are purely evangelical and spiritual. The Christian has free access to those three subordinate sources of pleasure, from which the men of the world derive the whole amount of their happiness; while at the same time, he has access to another source of enjoyment better than either of these, suited to the nature of man, less liable to be interrupted, and more refined, from which they are cut off by their unbelief. It is not, however, doing justice to the Christian to represent him as merely on an equality with the men of the world respecting the pleasure derived from these inferior sources: the point we conceive, is capable, not of mathematical demonstration, indeed, but of illustration and proof, satisfactory to every candid mind, that he enjoys a greater degree of happiness from these sources than other men do, or than he would do if he did not possess the Christian character. The truth of this position, as it relates to animal pleasure, will, no doubt, appear the most questionable. On this subject a few remarks will, therefore, be offered.

We must suppose the Christian, in all other respects, to be equal to those with whom he is compared; he is to possess the same wealth with them, or they are to be surrounded with the same indigence and want with him; they are to enjoy the same degree of health, or suffer the same affliction. Besides, in speaking of human happiness, our view must not be confined to a single day, or an hour; but the whole period of life must be included. Temporary pain is often endured for the sake of future and lasting good; and temporary pleasure is often productive of long protracted pain. Those temporary pains which prolong the period of life, increase, of course, the amount of happiness; and those pleasures which shorten this period, of course, diminish this amount. It must be remembered also that religion does not change the natural appetites, belonging to man. Because the Christian loves and obeys God, his taste is not, therefore, blunted or destroyed. He will, of course, derive as much pleasure from this source as they can. He is permitted to enjoy all the good things of this world, within the bounds of moderation; which bounds are laid down in the Bible. All beyond these limits is inconsistent with happiness, and is therefore prohibited. On this part of the subject, we refer to remarks already offered respecting *intemperance*, which is, in the enjoyment of sensual pleasure, the transgression of these bounds. There are, however, not a few men of the world who are temperate in all these pleasures: has the Christian any advantage over these?

If you should receive from a highly respected and beloved friend, something, suppose of no great value in itself, but as the evidence and pledge of your mutual friendship, and as the memorial of his affection for you; would not this circumstance very much enhance its value, in your estimation? Would not the possession and enjoyment of this article give you much greater pleasure than if you had accidentally found it, or even obtained it by your exertions? If obtained by your own exertions, its intrinsic value would have been precisely the same; but the pleasure you derive from it is not proportioned to this abstract value, but chiefly to that friendship and affection, of which it is the evidence and the memorial. Now this, in a degree, however, much more interesting, is the circumstance under which the Christian enjoys the blessings of this world. He feels and he acknowledges that he is a sinner; and of course that he does not deserve these blessings. He acknowledges also that they are unmerited favours, bestowed on him by his heavenly Father. He receives them as evidences of the love, the mercy, the forbearance, the compassion of God towards him. They remind him of this love and this mercy; hence they awaken his gratitude and love to God, *the giver of every good and perfect gift.* He does not receive them as accidentally thrown in his way, or as the result of his own exertions; though these exertions may have been used for this purpose; but as sent to him, on the tide of Providence according to the special design of infinite wisdom. The daily bread which nourishes him; the clothing which protects him; that health, which is the basis of all earthly happiness, will be enjoyed, not merely with that pleasure which arises from the gratification of appetite, but with a zest of delightful feeling, with a glow of gratitude and love, called forth by the reception of these blessings. "This bread," he will say, "is a gift from my heavenly Father; is a proof that he still loves me, the evidence that, unworthy as I am, he still loves me." He cannot, therefore, receive it as a mere animal gratification, but with the additional pleasure which this circumstance imparts to it. Now, although it is a fact, that these favours are bestowed on the men of the world, by the same kind Providence, yet they do not acknowledge the fact; they receive the gift, but forget the benefactor. To their own exertions, and to the operation of second causes, they refer their enjoyments; of course, there is no object of gratitude and love presented to their mind; their thoughts are led no farther than to themselves, and to the agency of natural causes: nothing meets their view calculated to excite these affections; the whole amount, therefore, of pleasure which they can taste, is sensual, derived from the gratification of appetite; the pleasure of the mere *animal man*. This the Christian enjoys in a degree equal with them; and has, in addition to this, the refined pleasure derived from a devout and grateful heart. Hence the declaration of the apostle: *every creature of God is good, and nothing to be refused,* emphatically GOOD, *if it be received with* THANKSGIVING.

Remarks already offered, and to which we refer, are intended to show that the Christian enjoys a greater degree of intellectual pleasure than others. We also refer to some of the preceding observations as proof that he enjoys a greater degree than others, of that pleasure which we call moral, to distinguish it from that which is pious and spiritual. All the moral virtues, and all the friendly and social affections, are required of the Christian, by motives much more forcible than those which operate on the minds of men who are *alienated from God.*

In this investigation, the medical effects of our passions and affections are too obvious and too important to be omitted.

Physicians of the present day generally ascribe the primary changes produced by the passions, to their influence upon the nervous power or grand principle of vitality, by which animated bodies are rendered susceptible of an infinite variety of impressions. In consequence of this influence, either the system in general, or some particular organ, is made to deviate from the exercise of those functions on which health depends; or is restored to its pristine office, after such deviations have taken place. Some of these passions, such as anger, wrath, resentment, &c., produce their effect by exciting to some excess through the power of their stimulus; others, such as fear, sorrow, &c., by inducing a temporary torpor and depression, disturb the animal functions; in the one case, by driving them into irregular haste by violent irritation; in the other, from their opposite effects, by causing them to move too slowly. These irregularities cannot fail to render the system more liable to disease, and have a tendency to shorten the period of life. Other affections, such as love, hope, gratitude, benevolence, &c., impart to the mind a cheerful though placid state of feeling, which produce a pleasing and salutary flow of the animal spirits, which has a tendency to preserve the health and prolong the life. It is worthy of remark, that those passions which have the most pernicious effect on our corporeal system, are those most frequently and clearly prohibited in scripture; and those which we are required to cherish are those which have the most salutary influence on human life, and, of course, on human happiness.

But although these effects are perceivable in a state of health, they are much more so in a state of sickness and debility: On this subject, that eminent physician, the late Dr. Rush, has given a proof of his wisdom, and accurate knowledge of the salutary or dangerous effect which the feelings and operations of the mind will have on the body. All who have read his Essays will remember the " Eagle's Nest." When the system is enervated, and especially when apprehensions of death are increasing, physicians, aware of the effect resulting from the least agitation or excitement, endeavour to keep the patient as quiet as possible; and this reason is sometimes alleged for discouraging religious exercises. If the patient has previously been accustomed to the devout exercise of the heart, this caution is unnecessary; such exercises will not injure him, but will most probably have a cheering effect on his spirits, and a salutary effect on the state of his health; if he has neglected the *one thing needful*, and has lived *without God in the world*, then by what means is he to be quieted? Can he suspend the exercise of thought? If not, can he confine his thoughts exclusively to the present, to the pain which he feels, the feebleness which prostrates him, the mournful sympathy of his friends? Can he be secured from all recollections of the past, and from all anticipations of the future? Can he quietly, and without fear, think of his past life; of the privileges he has neglected, of the mercies he has abused, of the number and aggravated nature of the sins he has committed against God, of that eternity into which he is about to be launched, of that judge in whose presence he is about to appear, of that sentence which will soon fix his everlasting condition? To think of these appalling subjects without fear and dread, requires a heart of adamant; not to think of them under such circumstances, implies an ignorance and stupidity which are indications of future anguish and despair. They may not intend it, but really the caution of some physicians, and of some friends, in such cases, is loud and solemn preaching. It enforces on us, like a voice from the grave, the warnings and declarations of the Bible: *Remember now thy Creator, in the days of thy youth, while the evil days come not, nor the years draw nigh, when thou shalt say, I have no pleasure in them: Behold, now is the accepted time; behold, now is the day of salvation: the night cometh, when no man can work.* It tells us that health is the time to prepare for eternity; that when sickness has prostrated us, when apprehensions of death are increasing every moment, it is then too late; that then the patient is not to be alarmed, but quieted and cheered, if possible, with the kindly influence of hope. But from whence is this hope to be derived? His life has been an uninterrupted scene of iniquity for which there is not a shadow of excuse; will this quiet his fears, and cheer him with hope? The jaws of death are just closing on him with their last tremendous crush; will this animate his spirits? Before him is the judgment-seat of Christ; will this give tranquillity and peace to his mind? No; but still his danger is to be kept out of his view, and he is to be amused with the hope of recovery. Sometimes this delusive amusement is continued till his connection with this world is for ever dissolved, and he is before his judge. The fact is, that if he thinks of these subjects, it is at the peril of his life; if he does not think of them, it is with the peril of his soul.

On the other hand: *Mark the perfect man, and behold the upright; for the end of that man is peace.* His faith in Christ secures the possession of this peace. *Being justified by faith we have peace with God, through our Lord Jesus Christ.* The dearest objects of his affections which he is leaving behind he can commend to the providence of his heavenly Father; his afflictions he bears with patience and resignation; the hope which he feels in a Saviour's death cheers and supports him; death itself will be gain to him; the Judge before whom he is to appear is that Redeemer whom he loves, and who has bought him with his blood. The pious affections of his heart will, therefore, preserve his mind in that state most favourable, if such should be the will of God, to his recovery. Nor does it require any artful disguise to feed the hope which quiets and cheers his mind; it is fed by the truth and mercy of God. The church may lament his loss; but he can rejoice in view of his eternal rest. His friends may weep around him; but he can triumph in the language of faith: *thanks be unto God who giveth me the victory.*

Our affections, it is well known, impart more or less of their own colouring to all objects with which we are connected. The mind of melancholy cast sees every thing dressed in the sable hue of its own complexion. The mind constitutionally cheerful will view the same objects clothed in more inviting colours. On this principle the pious affections of the Christian contribute not a little to the happiness of his life; a happiness which none but the Christian can enjoy. Love and hope are known to fill the mind with a steady and placid cheerfulness which imparts to every object a more pleasing aspect than that in which it would appear to a mind without these affections. That which is gloomy and distressing, is less so; that which is agreeable, is more so, through their benign influence.

In this way, can we not ascertain the meaning of that very remarkable promise of our Saviour: *Blessed are the meek, for they shall inherit the earth.* To inherit is to possess as our own. But the possession of the things of this world is valuable no farther than they contribute to our happiness. Divest them of this tendency, and the possession of them is of no value, they cease to be desirable or interesting to us. Those things which we do enjoy, from which we derive real happiness, are, in the same proportion, and for this very reason, our own; for they answer the only purpose for which possession is valuable. It is but little, compared with the whole, that we can enjoy, by the gratification of our appetites; for these appetites are limited; and satiety, disgust, and pain is the certain consequence of disregarding, or attempting to force, these limits. The Christian, in a legal sense, or according to the civil polity of his country, may possess but very little of this world; yet in another sense, it is all his own. He views it through the medium of his affections, and particularly of love, and sees it dressed in those pleasing colours which these affections impart to it; he derives less or more enjoyment from every part of it; and with propriety it may be said, he inherits all that he enjoys. The splendours of wealth which only feed the pride or gratify the vanity of the legal possessor, are, to the pious mind, a display of the divine munificence and glory; from this wealth, therefore, he derives a real pleasure, while that of the possessor may be only imaginary. If the earth, therefore, contributes to the happiness of the meek, it is their inheritance; an inheritance of which they cannot be deprived, unless they can be divested of their pious affections.

The Bible teaches us the true theory of human happiness; and if we are not very widely mistaken, experience confirms this theory. When happiness is analyzed, it will be found to depend far less on external circumstances than on the state of the mind. You may look at the splendid palace, adorned with every ornament, supplied with every convenience and comfort which wealth can procure, yet the inhabitants may be among the most miserable of mankind. Their appetites may be cloyed by repeated and excessive indulgence; their minds disquieted by pride, ambition, jealousy, and envy; torn and distracted by violent paroxysms of anger, by deep-rooted hatred, by implacable resentment; constantly agitated with discontent, impatience, fretfulness, and a host of similar feelings. Here are the means of such enjoyments as this earth can afford, but no real pleasure, no rational happiness. Visit, again, the cottage of the poor, without a single ornament, convenience, or comfort which indicate wealth; where every thing suggests the idea of poverty and want; yet the tenants of this cottage may be among the happiest of mankind. Here is contentment with the condition in which Providence has placed them; their scanty meals are received with gratitude, of course with real pleasure. This humble retreat is not invaded by the turbulence of guilty passions; meekness, humility, kindness, and charity, impart a mild and heavenly serenity. Here faith, and hope, and love, exert their influence in purifying the heart, in regulating the life, in raising the mind above this earth, and filling it with that joy and peace which flow from communion with God. The sun of worldly prosperity may visit them with but few of his rays; but the *sun of righteousness* warms and animates and cheers their souls with his heavenly beams. The favour of man may never smile upon them; but the favour of God, which is life, and his loving-kindness which is better than life, fills them with joy and peace. In the exercise of faith through the benign influence of hope and love they have a source of happiness within themselves, not liable to be affected by the perpetual flux and reflux which characterizes all earthly pleasures. If the rivulets of worldly enjoyment should be left dry; or, what is more, if they should flow with the bitter waters of affliction, they have, within themselves, a source of happiness which never fails. That river of life, which gladdens the city of God, flows with all its blessings into their hearts. The case is widely different with those who have no other source of enjoyment than this world. Every change in their circumstances will, of course, affect their happiness; one stroke of affliction will cut them off from their enjoyments. Nor have they, when thus separated from the world, any other resource from whence real happiness can be derived. The world is their portion; and when this is gone, they are left without relief from spiritual sources, to all the rude buffetings of adversity, and to all the corrodings of disappointed hopes and blasted expectations.

Whether that most excellent tract, The Shepherd of Salisbury Plain, be "No Fiction," or not, we will not undertake to decide; we are sure, however, that it is not romance. A more simple, natural, and touching narrative never flowed from an uninspired pen. Every shepherd, every man, however humble his station, however straitened his circumstances, however numerous and pressing his afflictions, might be what this shepherd was; a man of faith and prayer, a man of ardent and scriptural piety. This man exemplifies the power of the Bible in supporting and cheering the mind under afflictions, and filling it with undisturbed serenity and heavenly joy. He shows also the manner in which the Bible produces these effects; by exciting his faith, his hope, his love, and his gratitude; by habitually calling his thoughts from objects afflictive and discouraging, to those which were delightful and animating, from things visible and temporal to things spiritual and eternal. We hesitate not to affirm that this poor man, in his humble retreat, enjoyed more real happiness than the most wealthy man in the kingdom, without piety, could possibly do, not excepting even the monarch who reigned over him. Nay, we think it questionable whether the sun, which never sets on the British dominions, shines on a happier man than the Shepherd of Salisbury Plain. In offering this suggestion, we have not forgotten that some of the wealthy, and even some of the nobility of that empire are pious. In addition to their piety, they have the means of procuring those comforts of which the shepherd is deprived. He is, however, contented and cheerful, and happy with his coarse and scanty fare; they can be no more with their comforts and their delicacies. Appetite enables him to derive as great a degree of animal pleasure from his plain and simple meal, as they can from their accustomed provisions. There is very little difference, if any at all, between the enjoyment of animal pleasures, and perfect contentment without them. Would the presence of a little morsel of salt, or a mug of pure simple water on the table, or the prospect of a dry thatch over their heads, awaken in their hearts the same glow of grateful and joyful feeling which they did in his? If not, then, surely he has the advantage of them; he enjoys more happiness than they. In the catalogue of blessings for which they are thankful, these little things are overlooked; the providence of God has taught him to notice and to value them as distinct and important additions to his happiness.

We have, not unfrequently, visited the *house of mourning*, made such by death; and have listened to the language of grief on these occasions. With close attention, we have observed the different character which sound scriptural piety, or the want of it, will give to the unrestrained language of sorrow. We have seen the husband taking the last look of the companion of his bosom; a companion whom he loved more than he loved his God and his Saviour, more than any other object in existence. She was the chief source of his happiness. He had lived *without God in the world:* had not been in the habit of acknowledging the providence of God; of tracing his blessings or his afflictions back to the wise and good designs of a Father in heaven. His views extended no farther than his own agency, and that of a few natural causes which had forced themselves on his observation. He has heard of the name of a Saviour, and of salvation through him; but is as great a stranger to communion with God, and is as incapable of deriving support and consolation from the gospel and its rich provisions, as the very pagan who bows before the dumb idol. There is not in the wide world, nor indeed in the universe, a substitute for the loss he has sustained in the death of a once beloved wife; not a single object which can impart one cheering ray to his heart. Tell him of the virtues, the amiable qualities, of his late companion; you only open the wounds in his heart, drive deeper the poniard of grief into his bleeding soul: for you thereby render more vivid and distressing the conviction that she is gone, she is his no more. Tell him of the mercy, the compassion of God; of the wise and gracious designs of Providence in this painful bereavement; you speak a language perfectly unintelligible to him, which conveys no definite idea to his mind, and which, of course, can give him neither consolation nor support. The unbelief and impenitence of his heart repel these consolations, so well calculated to cheer and sustain the pious mind. The dark and cheerless suggestions of philosophy or of infidelity cannot reach his case, nor remove the deep anguish which has seated itself in his soul. No support is derived from tracing back his affliction to some designing, intelligent, and gracious cause; nor by viewing it connected with future and lasting benefit to himself: it springs, he knows not whence; it tends, he knows not whither. At this painful moment, his incoherent language, his violent exclamations, while they indicate the ardency of those affections now bereft of their object, and the agony of grief which he suffers, prove that he suffers without mitigation or relief, and that he knows not where to look for consolation and support. By one stroke of affliction the world has become to him a perfect blank; and unbelief and impiety have alienated his heart from that God who is *a refuge in distress, a very present help in trouble.*

We have seen, on the other hand, a mother, whose sensibility of heart has not been diminished, but refined and improved, by the influence of the Bible, imprinting the last solemn kiss on the lips of a beloved child, now cold in death; a child whose comparative innocence, whose tenderness, whose loveliness had entwined it with every fibre of the heart; a child which she had received as an important trust from God, to whom she devoutly commended it in prayer; over which she had often pondered with mingled emotions; sometimes with pleasing hopes of its future piety and usefulness to the church; sometimes with pensive apprehensions respecting the dark volume of futurity; at one time, rejoicing with it through scenes of prosperity and happiness; at another, recollecting the mutability of all sublunary prospects, the frailty and uncertainty of human life, clinging to it with unabated affection through seasons of adversity, with sleepless anxiety, watching, and soothing, and cherishing it through the last sad hours of sickness, pouring a mother's blessing on it, as the last struggle and the last breath announce the departure of the spirit, and then resigning it to the grave, and commending herself to the mercy of her God and her Saviour. These last mournful anticipations have proved to be prophetic; the last act of kindness, which maternal tenderness and affection could suggest, has been performed; from her eye is now flowing the parting tear; her bosom is now heaving the last adieu. The language which grief permits her to use, or by which grief seeks to assuage itself, proves that her distress is not less poignant, than it would have been, if the Bible had not impressed on her heart the image of the divine Saviour; but it proves also that her distress is directed and controlled, and that she is supported by the exercise of faith, and hope, and love. By the light of faith she traces back this affliction to a wise and holy design, which was formed in the counsels of infinite wisdom, and which existed in the Divine mind before the foundations of the world. She sees that this affliction, with all its circumstances, forms a part of a great plan, intended to prepare her for the joy of her Lord, for the rest and the bliss of heaven. With a firm, though humble confidence, she believes it will work for her good, and promote her spiritual advantage. She suffers, indeed, but not as an orphan, without sharing in the tenderest sympathies of friendship. She views the rod which afflicts her in the hand of fatherly compassion, every stroke of which is measured by love. Without one rebellious feeling, with meek and filial submission, she resigns herself and her child to God, using the language of an afflicted saint of old, *The Lord gave, and the Lord hath taken away;* and then adding with a peculiar emphasis, which nothing but piety in distress could give; *blessed be the name of the Lord!*

Few scenes are more impressive and useful, than to witness the Christian in affliction; blessing the hand that smites him; giving up, without a murmur, the dearest earthly object of affection; meeting the Saviour who approaches with his animating voice, on the waves of sorrow, which break all around him. Never does religion appear clothed in more lovely and heavenly attraction, than when calming the bosom, and cheering the spirit of the child of God, when suffering the correction of his heavenly Father. Let others, with thoughtless eagerness, rush to the house of feasting; partake of the sumptuous provision, collected from the four quarters of the globe; behold the splendours of wealth, and drown the reflections of death and eternity, amidst the pomp and the merriment of this world: lead me to the house of mourning, to witness the power of faith, and hope, and love, in comforting and sustaining the Christian under the pressure of affliction!

Such is the Bible; and such are the effects which it is producing; and such are the strong claims which it has on the patronage and zeal of all who are friends to the cultivation and improvement of the human intellect; friends to the good order, the peace, and prospeaity of society; friends to the real happiness of man; friends to the cause of God. The most rational consolation and support, the purest joy which man, in this vale of sorrow, can taste; the brightest days which this dark, and miserable, and sinful world will ever witness, will be owing to the influence of the Book of God. The most enrapturing delights, and the sublimest glories of heaven itself, will result from the influence of the gospel.

THE END

Solid Ground Complete Titles Listing
Newest Titles in Bold

Addresses to Young Men by Rev. Daniel Baker $16.00
Advice to a Young Christian by Jared B. Waterbury $15.00
The Afflicted Man's Companion by John Willison $20.00
Anecdotes: *Religious, Moral & Entertaining* by Charles Buck $28.00
Annals of the American Baptist Pulpit, W.B. Sprague $100.00 2 vols. (HC)
Annals of the American Presbyterian Pulpit, W.B. Sprague $215.00 3 vols. (HC)
Assurance of Faith, - Louis Berkhof $11.00
Backslider, The: *Nature, Symptoms & Recovery* by Andrew Fuller $13.00
Be Careful How You Listen: *Getting the Most out of the Sermon* by Jay Adams $16.00
Bible Animals: *And the Lessons Taught by Them for Children*, Richard Newton $16.00
Bible Jewels: *And the Lessons Taught by Them for Children*, Richard Newton $16.00
Bible Models: Shining Lights of Scripture by Richard Newton $32.00
Bible Promises: *Sermons for Children* by Richard Newton $17.00
Bible Warnings: *Sermons for Children* by Richard Newton $25.00
Biblical & Theological Studies, - Princeton Profs. (HC) $60.00 , (PB) $40.00
Body of Divinity by Archbishop James Ussher (HC) $50.00
Bow in the Cloud *Springs of Comfort in Affliction* by Buchanan, etc., $25.00
My Brother's Keeper: *Letters to a Younger Brother* – J.W. Alexander $13.00
Bunyan of Brooklyn: *Life and Practical Sermons of* Ichabod Spencer $30.00
Calvinism in History - Nathaniel McFetridge $13.00
Calvin Memorial Addresses – Warfield, Webb, Orr, Reed, D'Aubigne... $25.00
Calvin on Scripture & Divine Sovereignty by John Murray $12.00
Chief End of Man, The by John Hall $12.00
Child at Home, The - John S.C. Abbott $15.00
Child's Book on the Fall of Man, The by Thomas H. Gallaudet $11.00
Child's Book on Repentance, The by Thomas H. Gallaudet $13.00
Child's Book on the Sabbath by Horace Hooker $16.00
Child's Book on the Soul by Thomas H. Gallaudet $15.00
Christian Pastor, The *Office & Duty of* Stephen H. Tyng $14.00
Christian's Present for All Seasons: *Thoughts of Eminent Divines* - $38.00
The Christian Warfare by John Downame $45.00
Christ in Song - Compiled by Philip Schaff $40.00
Christ on Cross & The Lord our Shepherd – John Stevenson $40.00
Church of Christ: In Two Volumes by James Bannerman $75.00
Church Members Guide – John Angell James $16.00 pb.; $27.00 hc.
Classic Reformed Discourses & Essays by J.H. Merle D'Aubigne $30.00
Phone 205-443-0311 – www.solid-ground-books.com

Check website for our latest discounts

For Whom Did Christ Die? *The Extent of the Atonement* by John Murray $5.00
Friendship: The Master Passion by H. Clay Trumbull $25.00
From the Flag to the Cross: *Civil War Stories* by A.S. Billingsley, $34.00
From the Pulpit to the Palm-Branch: *Memorial to Spurgeon* $25.00
From Toronto to Emmaus: *Empty Tomb Skepticism to Faith* by James White $17.00
Gadsby's Hymns: *Selections of Hymns for Worship* by William Gadsby $20.00
Gentleman and a Scholar – J. A. Broadus (HC) $40.00; (PB) $30.00
Golden Hours: *Heart-Hymns of the Christian Life*– Elizabeth Prentiss $10.00
Good, Better, Best: *Classic Work on Ministry to the Poor* by J.W. Alexander $17.00
Grace and Glory: *Sermons from Chapel at Princeton Seminary* Geerhardus Vos $15.00
Harmony of the Divine Attributes *in the Work of Redemption* by Wm Bates $28.00
Hawker's Poor Man's N.T. Commentaries (HC) (3 vols.) $195.00
Hawker's Poor Man's O.T. Commentaries (HC) (6 vols.) $395.00
Hawker's Poor Man's Bible Dictionary (HC) by Robert Hawker $55.00
Heart for Missions, A: *Life of Samuel Pearce* by Andrew Fuller $17.00
Heaven Upon Earth: *Jesus, Best Friend in Worst Times,* James Janeway $23.00
Heroes of the Early Church by Richard Newton $17.00
Heroes of Israel: *Abraham – Moses* by William G. Blaikie $35.00
Heroes of the Reformation: *Lessons for Young* by Richard Newton - $20.00
History of Christian Doctrine (2 vols) by William G.T. Shedd $62.00
History of Preaching (HC) (2 vols.) - Edwin C. Dargan $115.00
History of the Sufferings of the Church of Scotland – Robert Wodrow $250.00
Homiletics and Pastoral Theology – William G.T. Shedd $22.00
The Humanness of John Calvin by Richard Stauffer $13.00
Imago Christi: *The Example of Christ* – James Stalker $18.00
The Influence of the Bible on Mind & Character by John Matthews $18.00
Is the Mormon my Brother? By James R. White $20.00
Italian Reformer, The: *Aonio Paleario* by W.M. Blackburn $23.00
JEREMIAH: A Parable of Jesus by Douglas Webster $15.00
Jesus and I are Friends: *Life of J.R. Miller* – John Faris $19.00
Jesus of Nazareth: *Character, Teachings & Miracles* by John Broadus $11.00
Jesus the Way: *A Child's Guide to Heaven* – Edward Payson Hammond $11.00
Jewish Tabernacle: *In Its Typical Teaching* by Richard Newton $25.00
King's Highway, The: *10 Commandments for the Young* R. Newton $20.00
Lectures on the Acts of the Apostles by John Dick $32.00
Lectures on the Bible to the Young by John Eadie $16.00
Lectures on the Book of Esther by Thomas M'Crie $25.00
Lectures on the History of Preaching – John A. Broadus $19.00
Lectures on the Law and the Gospel by Stephen Tyng $25.00
Phone 205-443-0311 – www.solid-ground-books.com

Check website for our latest discounts

Our Sovereign God by Boice, Packer, Stott, Sproul, Nicole $16.00
Pardon and Assurance by William J. Patton $20.00
Pastor in the Sickroom – John Wells $13.00
A Pastor's Counsel by Jonathan Edwards, Thomas Scott etc. $12.00
Pastor's Daughter, The – Louisa Payson Hopkins $16.00
Pastor's Sketches: Double-Volume Work– Ichabod Spencer $35.00
Pathway into the Psalter by William Binnie $30.00
Paul the Preacher: *Discourses in Acts* by John Eadie $30.00
Person and Work of the Holy Spirit, The – B.B. Warfield $12.00
The Power of the Pulpit by Gardiner Spring $20.00
Power of God Unto Salvation – B.B. Warfield PB - $18.00; HC $32.00
Preacher and His Models, The – James Stalker $19.00
Precious Seed: *Discourses by Scottish Worthies* by Brown, Chalmers, $32.00
Princeton Sermons from 1891-92 by Hodge, Warfield, Patton etc.
Publications of the American Tract Society, 6 vols. $175.00
Preparation and Delivery of Sermons: *Dargan Edition* – J.A. Broadus $35.00
Psalms in History and Biography, The by John Ker $18.00
Psalms in Human Life by Roland Prothero $25.00
Pulpit Crimes: *Criminal Mishandling of God's Word* by James White $17.00
Rays from the Sun of Righteousness: *Sermons for Children* by Richard Newton $17.00
Redeemer's Tears Wept Over the Lost, The by John Howe $11.00
Repentance & Faith: *Explained to the Young* by Charles Walker $16.00
Sabbath Scripture Readings: *New Testament* by Thomas Chalmers $32.00
Sabbath Scripture Readings II – Old Testament by Thomas Chalmers $35.00
Safe Compass and How it Points: *Sermons to Children* by Richard Newton, $16.00
Scottish Pulpit, The – William M. Taylor $19.00
Scientific Investigation of the Old Testament by Robert Dick Wilson $18.00
Scripture Biography for the Young: Vols. 1 - 5 by T.H. Gallaudet $95.00
Scripture Biography for the Young: King Josiah by T.H. Gallaudet $12.00
Scripture Guide, The – J.W. Alexander $18.00
Secret of Communion with God – Matthew Henry $12.00
Secrets of Happy Home Life by J.R. Miller $5.00
SEEKING GOD: *Do You Really Want to Know God?* by Peter Jeffery $5.00
Sermons for Christian Families by Edward Payson $20.00
Sermons to the Natural Man – William G.T. Shedd $24.00
Sermons to the Spiritual Man– William G.T. Shedd $24.00
Shepherd's Heart, A – Pastoral Sermons of J.W. Alexander $28.00
A Short Explanation of Hebrews by David Dickson $13.00
Shorter Catechism Illustrated by John Whitecross PB - $15.00; HC $25.00
Phone 205-443-0311 – www.solid-ground-books.com

Check website for our latest discounts

Come Ye Apart: *Thoughts from Gospels* – J.R. Miller $25.00
Commentaries on Galatians-Thess. By John Eadie $145.00 (5 vols)
Commentary on Hebrews by William Gouge, $115 hc, $85.00 pb (2 vols.)
Commentaries on Joshua, 1 & 2 Samuel by William G. Blaikie $92.00 (3 vols)
Commentary on the Epistle to the Romans by W.G.T. Shedd $32.00
Commentary on the New Testament by John Trapp $80.00
Commentary on the Pastoral Epistles by C.J. Ellicott $20.00
Commentary on Second Peter by Thomas Adams HC $90.00
Commenting and Commentaries by C.H. Spurgeon $16.00
Common Faith, Common Culture by Joseph Bianchi $16.00
Communicant's Companion, The by Matthew Henry $20.00
Decisional Regeneration vs. Divine Regeneration by J.E. Adams $8.00
Devotional Life of a Sunday School Teacher, The – J.R. Miller $12.00
Divine Love, The: *12 Sermons on God's Love* by John Eadie $28.00
The Divine Purpose *Displayed in Providence & Grace* by John Matthews $16.00
The Doctrine of Endless Punishment by W.G.T Shedd $15.00
Doctrine of Justification by James Buchanan $35.00
Doctrine of Sovereign Grace Opened & Vindicated by Isaac Backus $15.00
Duties of Church Members & Plea to Pray for Pastors by James & Spring $5.00
Early Piety Illustrated: *Memoir of Nathan Dickerman* by Gorham Abbott $11.00
Evangelical Truth: *Sermons for the Family*– Archibald Alexander $36.00
The Excellent Woman: *As Portrayed in Proverbs* – Anne Pratt $20.00
Exposition of the Baptist Catechism by Benjamin Beddome $17.00
Exposition of the Epistle of Jude by William Jenkyn $55.00 (hc)
An Exposition of the Ten Commandments by Ezekiel Hopkins $28.00
Expository Discourses on the Book of Genesis by Andrew Fuller $40.00
Expository Lectures on Ruth and Esther by George Lawson $25.00
Family Worship for the Christmas Season by Ray Rhodes $12.00
Family Worship for the Reformation Season by Ray Rhodes $12.00
Family Worship for the Thanksgiving Season by Ray Rhodes $12.00
Famous Missionaries of the Reformed Church by James I. Good
Famous Reformers of the Reformed & Presbyterian Church by J.I. Good
Famous Women of the Reformed Church by James I. Good $22.00
The Family at Home: *Illustrations of Domestic Duties* by Gorham Abbott $25.00
The Fear of God: *The Soul of Godliness* by John Murray $5.00
Feed My Lambs: *Lectures to Children* by John Todd $15.00
First Things: *Discourses from Genesis* – Gardner Spring $50.00
Five Points of Calvinism by Robert L. Dabney $10.00
Forgotten Heroes of Liberty, The by J.T. Headley $27.00
Phone 205-443-0311 – www.solid-ground-books.com

Check website for our latest discounts

Lectures on Revivals of Religion by William B. Sprague $25.00

Legacy of a Legend: *Spiritual Treasure from the Heart of Edward Payson* $10.00

Let the Cannon Blaze Away by Joseph P. Thompson $23.00

Letters to a Mormon Elder by James R. White $20.00

The Life & Letters of James Henley Thornwell by Benjamin M. Palmer $60.00

The Life & Letters of James Renwick: Scots Martyr by WH Carslaw $20.00

Life and Sermons of Ichabod Spencer (HC) (3 vols.) $120.00

Life of Jesus Christ for the Young by Richard Newton $65.00 (2 vols.)

Light at Evening Time: *Support & Comfort of the Aged* $25.00

Little Pillows and Morning Bells by Francis Havergal $16.00

Lives, Our Fortunes & Our Sacred Honor, Our by Charles Goodrich $30.00

Log College: *Accounts from the Great Awakening* by Archibald Alexander $20.00

Lord of Glory: *Classic Defense of the Deity of Christ* - B.B. Warfield $18.00

Luther's Scottish Connection by James McGoldrick 17.00

Madison Ave. Lectures on Baptist Principles & Practice by Weston $25.00

The Man of Business by J.W. Alexander, W.B. Sprague, John Todd etc. $20.00

A Manual for the Young: *Exposition of Proverbs 1-9* by Charles Bridges $13.00

The Marrow of True Justification by Benjamin Keach $12.00

Martyrland: *A Tale of the Covenanters* by Robert Simpson $20.00

Mary Bunyan: *Faith of the Blind Daughter of John Bunyan* by S.R. Ford $20.00

Memorial Tributes: *Funeral Addresses* by Spurgeon, Newton, Jay $35.00

The Minister and His Greek New Testament by A.T. Robertson $14.00

The Missionary Enterprise: 15 Discourses, edited by Baron Stow, $23.00

The Mission of Sorrow: *God's Purpose in Afflictions* by Gardiner Spring $11.00

More Love to Thee: *Life of Elizabeth Prentiss* – GL Prentiss (PB) $35.00; HC $50.00

Mothers of the Wise and Good - Jabez Burns $16.00

Mother at Home, The – John S.C. Abbot $15.00

Mourning a Beloved Shepherd – Charles Hodge & John Hall $10.00

Morning Stars: *Names of Christ for His Little Ones* by Francis Havergal $12.00

My Mother: *Recollections of Maternal Influence* – John Mitchell $20.00

National Preacher, The – Edited by Austin Dickinson $23.00

Notes, Critical & Explanatory on the Acts of the Apostles by Jacobus $32.00

Notes on Galatians by J. Gresham Machen $20.00

Nuts for Boys to Crack: *Earthly Stories w/ Heavenly Meaning* by John Todd $20.00

Old Paths for Little Feet – Carol Brandt $13.00

Opening Scripture: *Hermeneutical Manual* – P.Fairbairn HC $50.00; PB $35.00

Opening Up Ephesians Peter Jeffery $9.00

Origin of Paul's Religion, The by J. Gresham Machen $24.00

Orthodoxy and Heterodoxy: *Writings on Theology & Ethics* – W.G.T. Shedd $23.00

Phone 205-443-0311 – www.solid-ground-books.com

Check website for our latest discounts

Small Talks on Big Questions: by Helms & Thompson-Kahler $32.00
Soldier's Catechism: *For US Armed Forces* by Michael Cannon $15.00
Southern Presbyterian Pulpit: *Expository Sermons* by Dabney, Hoge, Palmer $30.00
Speaking the Truth in Love: *Life of Roger Nicole* by David Bailey $34.00
The Sovereignty of God by John Murray, John Macleod et. $18.00
Stepping Heavenward (HC) – Elizabeth Prentiss $25.00
Stepping Heavenward Study Guide – Carson Kistner $14.00
Still Hour, The: *Communion with God in Prayer* by Austin Phelps $12.00
Sunday School Teachers Guide – John Angell James $11.00
Theology on Fire: 1 & 2 – Sermons of J.A. Alexander $28.00 each
THEOLOGY: *Explained & Defended* by Timothy Dwight $225.00 set (4 vols) HC
Theological Interpretation of American History by C. Gregg Singer $25.00
Thoughts on Preaching by James W. Alexander $22.00
The Tract Primer: *First Lessons in Sound Doctrine* by American Tract Society $11.00
Transfigured Life, The: *Selected Shorter Writings of JR Miller* $25.00
The Travels of True Godliness by Benjamin Keach $17.00
Truth About Christmas, The – Peter Jeffery $4.00
Truth & Life: *22 Christ-Centered Sermons* by Charles P. McIlvaine $30.00
Truth Made Simple: *Attributes of God for Children* by John Todd $15.00
The TRUTH Set Us Free: 20 Nuns Tell Their Stories by Richard Bennett $16.00
Two Men from Malta: *Passionate Appeal to Roman Catholics* by Joe Serge $15.00
An Undivided Love*: Loving and Living for Christ* by Adolphe Monod $15.00
What is the Kingdom of God? By R.C. Reed $12.00
Whatsoever Things Are True: *Discourses on Truth* – J.H. Thornwell $16.00
Withhold Not Thine Hand: *Evening Sermons* by William Jay $35.00
Woman: Her Mission and Life – Adolphe Monod $12.00
Word and Prayer, The: *Devotions from the Minor Prophets*– John Calvin $11.00
The Workman: *His False Friends & True Friends* by Joseph P. Thompson $20.00
Work of the Ministry, The – William G. Blaikie - $22.00
THE WORKS OF THOMAS MANTON (22 vols) HC $1,000.00
Yearning to Breathe Free? *Immigration, Islam & Freedom* by David Dykstra $16.00
Young Ladies Guide – Harvey Newcomb $22.00
Young Peoples' Problems by J.R. Miller $16.00
Youth's Book on Natural Theology by Thomas H. Gallaudet $18.00

Phone 205-443-0311 – www.solid-ground-books.com

AUDUBON PRESS TITLES
Now Solid Ground Christian Books

The following 14 titles have been purchased from Audubon Press, and are being offered at a standard **40% discount.**

AS THE WATERS COVER THE SEA: *Millenial Expectations in the Rise of Anglo-American Missions 1640-1810*
by James A. De Jong
> List Price $28.00 – SGCB Price $16.80

THE BELIEVER'S EXPERIENCE
Maintaining the Scriptural Balance between Experience and Truth
Erroll Hulse
> List Price $20.00 – SGCB Price $12.00

CHRIST'S GLORIOUS KINGDOM
Postmillenialism Reconsidered
John Jefferson Davis
> List Price $20.00 – SGCB Price $12.00

COME, LET US REASON TOGETHER
The Sufficiency of Christ and the Unity of the Church - Jews & Gentiles Together
Baruch Maoz
> List Price $20.00 – SGCB Price $12.00

FORTY YEARS FAMILIAR LETTERS:
The Life & Letters of J.W. Alexander (two volumes)
John Hall
> List Price $60.00 – SGCB Price $36.00

THE GREAT INVITATION
Examining the Use of the Altar Call in Evangelism
Erroll Hulse
> List Price $20.00 – SGCB Price $12.00

AN INTRODUCTION TO THE BAPTISTS
Erroll Hulse
> List Price $15.00 – SGCB Price $9.00

205-443-0311 — www.solid-ground-books.com

THE LIFE AND TIMES OF GARDINER SPRING
In Two Volumes
Gardiner Spring
    List Price $60.00 – SGCB Price $36.00

The Life of J.A.Alexander
In Two Volumes
Henry Carrington Alexander
    List Price $60.00 – SGCB Price $36.00

The New York City Prayer Revival of 1858 and Its Lessons J.W. Alexander
    List Price $20.00 – SGCB Price $12.00

The New York Pulpit During The Prayer Revival of 1858 J.W. Alexander
    List Price $28.00 – SGCB Price $16.80

A PROPHET ON THE RUN
A Devotional Commentary on the Book of Jonah
Baruch Maoz
    List Price $15.00 – SGCB Price $9.00

PULLING THE EYE TOOTH FROM A LIVE TIGER: *A Memoir of the Life and Labors of Adoniram Judson (in two volumes)* by Francis Wayland
    List Price $75.00 – SGCB Price $45.00

THEOLOGY OF MISSIONS IN THE PURITAN TRADITION
A Study of Representative Puritans: Richard Sibbes, Richard Baxter, John Eliot, Cotton Mather & Jonathan Edwards
Sidney H. Rooy
    List Price $32.00 – SGCB Price $19.20

205-443-0311 — www.solid-ground-books.com

www.ingramcontent.com/pod-product-compliance
Lightning Source LLC
Chambersburg PA
CBHW022125080426
42734CB00006B/241